Americans are trapped in a dysfunctiona[...] ly chants its mantra: *"You can have ever[...] you want as long as you have enough credit!"* You can have the sixty inch flat panel TV from the big box store, the new SUV, the dream vacation, the lavish "it-only-happens-once-in-a-lifetime" wedding, the upscale home in the hottest new neighborhood, a perfect retirement, and on and on and on…

To this way of thinking "I can afford it," really means you have enough income to make the payments — including huge amounts of interest. It *whispers* that you only get to use the things you "buy;" that you really don't own them. But, it *shouts* that just "having" them proves your wealth and worth. This model is designed to make others wealthy at your expense. It makes bad decisions feel good.

This model is called the Debt Paradigm.

And, when some life event decimates your income and Debt Paradigm decisions dump you into a dungeon of despair, some "credit repair" guy slithers from the shadows to show you the way out of the darkness and back into the light of this failed model — so you can do it all again.

There is a better way. *Money for Life* shows you how to take control of the money that flows through your life without giving up your lifestyle. *Money for Life* works for you *in good times and bad.* Job loss, disability, illness, family crisis — or any other life event that could throw you for a loss — becomes manageable.

Money for Life lets you look forward with confidence *in good times and bad,* so you never have to look back with regret.

Read on…

Money for Life!

...in good times and bad

This book is given as a legacy to

_____

from

_____

Money for Life!

...in good times and bad

You Be The Bank .com

Jeffrey Reeves, MA
with
Dr Agon Fly

Money for Life!
...in good times and bad

Poor Richard Publishing Co.
Denver, CO

By Dr Agon Fly with Jeffrey Reeves, MA
All Rights Reserved © 2008 by Poor Richard Publishing Co.

For information, contact Poor Richard Publishing, 1270 Jasmine St., Denver CO 80220 – (303)355-0550 – Dr_Agon_Fly@YouBeTheBank.com.

Published by Poor Richard Publishing Co.
Printed in the United States of America
1st Printing

Author: Dr Agon Fly with Jeffrey Reeves, MA
Editor: Travitt Hamilton – The Write Stuff

13-digit ISBN: 978-0-9797709-0-6
10-digit ISBN:0-9797709-0-4

Library of Congress Control Number :2007908616

This publication is designed to provide accurate and informative information with regard to the subject matter covered. It is sold with the understanding that the publisher is not engaged in rendering legal, accounting, or other professional advice. If legal advice or other expert assistance is required, the services of a competent professional person should be sought.

— From a Declaration of Principles jointly adopted by a Committee of the American Bar Association and a Committee of Publishers and Associations

For bulk purchases or more information please call 1-888-300-9661
Dr_Agon_Fly@YouBeTheBank.com

Graphic Design: Sandra Reeves of Poor Richard Publishing Co.
Caricature: Robert Bauer of www.goofyfaces.com

Dedication and
Acknowledgments

"...Nothing comes from nothing. Nothing ever could. So somewhere in my youth or childhood – I must have done something good..." ~ The Sound of Music

T he words in this book flow from the experience of 67 years...

☞ nearly fifty years owning and operating businesses or bits and pieces of businesses (some successful and some failed enterprises) as diverse as coal mining in Appalachia, software development and systems consulting, and a professional sports team (God forgive me for that one.)

☞ over thirty years as a licensed life insurance agent (some of them as a reluctant registered securities representative) and as the owner and operator of an insurance and financial advisory practice...one of the successes.

It equally derives from...

☞ the wisdom of the Torah
☞ Martin Buber's *I and Thou*
☞ Thomas 'A Kempis's *The Imitation of Christ*
☞ the teachings of the Buddha Siddhartha Gautama
☞ the spiritual guidance of Rabbi Zalman Schachter-Shalomi and Father "Archie" of the Comboni Missionaries
☞ Benjamin Franklin's writings — especially *The Art of Virtue* and *The Way to Wealth*

- ☞ *The Four Agreements* by Don Miguel Ruiz
- ☞ George S. Clason's *The Richest Man in Babylon*
- ☞ the inspiration and teachings of Bill and Tom Newman, developers of the PACE Seminar and among the founders of the Human Potential Movement
- ☞ the writings of Napoleon Hill, Dale Carnegie and many others who have contributed to the human potential movement
- ☞ the encouragement of Bill Fanning and Sister Francine of McNicholas High School, Cincinnati, OH
- ☞ and too many other mentors and teachers to mention.

There is a consistent influence running through those 67 years like a vein of gold appearing and receding in a mine tunnel. It is the use of teaching as a way of giving to others and earning an income in the process...

- ☞ teaching grade school, junior high school and college
- ☞ coaching high school athletics
- ☞ teaching migrant workers
- ☞ instructing US Air Force officers and civil servants
- ☞ developing and conducting goal setting and time management seminars for Fortune 100 companies
- ☞ creating and executing training programs for businesses
- ☞ conducting pre-licensing and continuing education courses for financial professionals
- ☞ creating and presenting numerous financial seminars for clients and the general public

Many individuals, from family to foreigner, have helped me along the way. I owe a significant debt to each of them for their influence, support, criticism, and antagonism. They have helped me clarify my role as a teacher and guide, and that has helped form the ideas in this book into a coherent message.

I would like to dedicate this book to those many individuals that have encouraged my successes and awakened me to my failures. Most especially, however, I dedicate this work to my wife and partner

Sandra Case-Reeves

who has supported every idea I've ever shown her just long enough to get out her 2x4 and show me why it is one of the dumbest ideas I ever had.

Fortunately, she thought this book was a good idea and I would not have completed it without her help and support.

Warning and Disclaimer

This book offers information and illustrations that are intended to be educational. It does not contain legal, financial, or other professional advice. Individuals requiring such services should consult a competent professional.

The author and publisher make no representations about the suitability of the information contained in this book for any purpose. This material provided "as is" without warranty of any kind.

Although every effort has been made to ensure the accuracy of the contents of this book, errors and omissions can occur. The publisher assumes no responsibility for any damages arising from the use of this book, or alleged to have resulted in connection with this book.

This book is not endorsed by any of the companies mentioned in the text.

Table of Contents

Foreword

You are holding in your hands a dangerous document.

On the surface, it appears to be a personal finance book, and in a sense it is. It addresses such issues as how you manage your money and what you use it for. The consequences of your answers to these questions reach into every aspect of your life. And, if you follow the tenets of *Money for Life*, you find the magic of compounding working for you to create life-long wealth that you can pass along to your children and grandchildren, and even more importantly, you find yourself in a position to pass wisdom along to them as well.

So, in one sense, this is a very practical book, with tactics that help you to set achievable goals and measure your progress toward reaching them, not that much different in some ways than a thousand personal finance books that came before it and a thousand books yet to come.

But *Money for Life...in good times and bad* is so much more than that, and therefore, so much more powerful than most of those other books. *Money for Life* demands that you look to the past in order to see a clear path into the future. It expects that you'll remember that the Money Monsters and the Behemoths work for you, and not the other way around (you'll meet these whimsical characters as you read the book).

Most importantly, it challenges you to connect your decisions about your money to your philosophy of life. If you think deeply about the book as you work through the practical, tactical exercises, you'll find yourself rethinking your relationship with money, and by extension, with the whole economy.

Aristotle, in his work *Nicomachean Ethics*, probed the question of what the ultimate good is. He had this to say about wealth: "The money-maker's life is in a way forced on him; and clearly wealth is not the good we are seeking, since it is useful, only for some other end."[1] For Aristotle, the other end is the "good life," which includes security and independence, as well as civic virtue and public service.

There is a modern strain of this kind of thought as well. It can be found in recent discussions of "positive psychology."[2] This is the term used by the American Psychological Association to describe the study of what makes people happy.

A recent paper describes the progress that has been made in understanding "positive psychology." The authors studied people who described themselves as happy, to find out if they had common characteristics. Using a combination of questionnaires, surveys, interviews and human subject reports, they find "...six overarching virtues that almost every culture across the world endorses: wisdom, courage, humanity, justice, temperance, and transcendence."[3] The

---

1 Aristotle. Nicomachaen Ethics. Terence Irwin, Ed. Indianapolis, Indiana: Hackett Publishing Company, Inc. 1985. p. 8.

2 Seligman, Martin E. P., Tracy A Steen, Nansook Park, and Christopher Peterson. "Positive Psychology Progress: Empirical Validation of Interventions." American Psychologist. Vol. 60, No. 5, July-August 2005. p. 410-421 Most of what follows relies heavily on this article.

3 Ibid.,p.411.

authors describe three robust, apparently universal empirical findings. For our purposes, the third finding is the most relevant. They write

> "[S]trengths "of the heart" — zest, gratitude, hope, and love — are more robustly associated with life satisfaction than are the more cerebral strengths such as curiosity and love of learning. We find this pattern among adults and among youths as well as longitudinal evidence that these "heart" strengths foreshadow subsequent life satisfaction."[4]

This is quite a different view of people than that taught in economics! Economists start by assuming that rationality and self-interest are the best way of understanding why people make the decisions they make (as if people only made rational decisions!) Consumer choice theory assumes that people derive utility (defined as well being, satisfaction, happiness, or whatever) only from consumer goods. Of course, most economists recognize that there are limits to this view, but nonetheless this is the view at the heart of most discussions of trade, and is not far below the surface in most other discussions.

The economic point is that how you spend or manage your money can be thought of as an extension of your deepest self, your core values. And this realization lies at the core of the *Money for Life* philosophy. When the choices you make with your money are in alignment with your deepest values, your money and the decisions you make regarding it are more likely to make you happy. Your money, and the Economy is serving you and the ideals you hold dear, not vice versa.

Money for Life also serves as a financial self-defense manual. My daughter's jujitsu instructor emphasizes the concept of situational awareness and the role it plays in preventing trouble. If you pay close

---

4   Ibid.,p.412.

attention to what is going on around you, you avoid problems. You can anticipate and prepare. The same can be said of your financial dealings. Prudent people can and do set aside money for contingencies. *Money for Life* helps you focus on what is going on around you, and plan for the best and the worst.

Jeffrey Reeves asked me to write this foreword a year and a half ago, and I told him I would have to think about it. And the reason I decided the answer would be yes is that Jeff and I are both ultimately on the side of Aristotle regarding the utility of wealth. The acquisition of personal wealth is well and good, and this book is an excellent guide to that pursuit.

But *Money for Life* is more than that, it is a timely reminder that the personal and national economic gains that this pursuit engenders should be working for each of us in good times and bad and not the other way around.

And that idea is what makes this book so dangerous and so valuable.

As Dr. Agon Fly says, "Read on…"

John Jeffrey Zink, Ph.D., Economics

Preface – The Money Monsters and the Behemoths

We live with three Money Monsters and hundreds of Behemoths every day. Each survives and thrives by consuming your money for its own benefit. Each is relentless and insatiable. Each has the power to consume all of your money.

The first Money Monster is fearsome and unforgiving — The Dragon makes no requests, only demands. If you deny this Money Monster its claims, it sinks its talons into your flesh and hangs on for as long as it takes to wrench from you the money it wants.

The second Money Monster is seductive — The Siren lures you with promises of wealth and success and happiness until you find yourself in its clutches and discover that the promises are all fantasies and the end game is to entrap you and drain you of all of your money.

The third Money Monster is ruthlessly patient — The Venus Flytrap waits — sometimes for decades — to ensnare you and suck as much of your money as it can from you in the shortest time possible. This Money Monster has a voracious appetite and can gobble up a lifetime of savings in just a few short months.

The Behemoths spend billions of your dollars each year convincing you to use borrowed money to buy things that promise to make you thin, rich, and happy but which ultimately impoverish you and make them wealthy.

Each of these Money Monsters is a familiar bureaucracy and each Behemoth is a familiar business. Each has a legitimate role in our society and in your life. Each can benefit you if you know how to circumvent its snares, avoid its pitfalls, recognize its ruses, and defuse its subterfuge. You cannot, however, ignore even one of these Money Monsters or Behemoths without the direst of consequences. You can, however, control your relationship with them.

Introducing Dr Agon Fly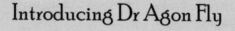

Dr Agon Fly is your guide and spokesperson throughout this book. He speaks for the professionals who advocate for the principles and practices this book promotes and for the many individuals who embrace those practices.

Dr Agon Fly is real. He is not a flesh and blood person like you and me, but he embodies the hundreds and thousands of women and men who have contributed to the development — over decades, centuries and millennia — of the humanizing and empowering ideas and values that you encounter as you explore *Money for Life*.

When Dr Agon Fly speaks to you he echos these voices:

- ☞ voices that have presented the same message for eons
- ☞ voices that have survived disparagement, ridicule, and attack from charlatans and snake oil salesmen who would have you embrace their ideas so they could embrace your money

☞ voices that speak now to help you challenge and overcome the failed paradigm that ensnares so many Americans today.

Read on...

The Dragon

The Dragon is the tax bureaucracy in all of its various and nefarious manifestations: property taxes, sales taxes, fuel taxes, telecommunications taxes, taxes on utilities, excise taxes, import taxes, city, county, state and federal income taxes, and many, many more unnamed taxes. The Dragon is your friend as long as you feed it properly. The Dragon becomes your unrelenting nemesis if you fail it even once.

The Dragon is, however, the least powerful and least threatening of the three Money Monsters. It only reacts to failures. The Dragon has a predictable and well-defined diet. Its feeding times are specific and it does not demand that everyone feed it the same amount or with the same frequency.

Remember, taxes pay for police protection, fire protection, homeland security, roads, schools, social programs, and all of the good our governments do for us. You should be happy to pay the Dragon in exchange for all it does. At the same time, you do not want to pay more than your share, nor more than you must. If you have your own "bank" and you build significant stores of wealth in your "bank," the Dragon not only doesn't demand a tax on that wealth but also protects it from taxation and from other predators[5].

---

5 Not all financial vehicles that you can use as a "bank" provide the same level of protections from taxation. Consult your advisors — financial, legal, and tax — regarding your personal situation.

The best way to deal with the Dragon is, therefore, to build your own "bank." It is also helpful to hire a Good Accountant — or to be one — who understands and accepts those money practices. S/he can then make certain that you pay only the taxes you should and none that you should not. A Good Accountant has a symbiotic relationship with the Dragon. As long as the Dragon is around, the Good Accountant makes sure the Dragon is fed the minimum it needs.

The Siren or Seducer

The Sirens of Greek mythology are the competitors for your money in the financial bureaucracy: every lender from your credit union with a single location, to the monolithic holding companies that promise everything from basic banking to complete financial planning, to home loans, to insurance, to investments you can "buy" to make yourself wealthy. Your friendly local banker, insurance agent, and stockbroker are part of this bureaucracy. The 18 months same-as-cash deal at the furniture store, 0% interest from the carmaker's finance company, your credit card — perhaps the greatest seducer of all — and too many others to mention, sing the "siren songs" that seduce you.

There are some not-so-obvious entries in this category, too: your 401(k) investment options, stocks, bonds, mutual funds, investment real estate, bank certificates of deposit, gold and other precious metals, foreign currency exchanges, collectibles like coins or art or wine — well, maybe wine's OK — and various kinds of insurance.

This is the most ubiquitous of the three monsters. It permeates almost every aspect of our society and culture — even the Dragon accepts credit cards. You need much of what this multi-faceted Money Monster provides. You have to have places to put money. You need credit cards to secure hotels, airlines and rental cars. Insurance on cars is required by the state and on homes by mortgage companies. Your

401(k) money has to be somewhere. Short-term loans to banks (savings accounts and the certificates of deposit that you purchase with terms of 3 to 60 months) make sense on occasion.

Taming this Money Monster and turning off the seductive Siren Songs is, however, essential to your long-term survival and success.

There is only one way to accomplish this daunting task and that is by marrying into the Money Monster's "family" and becoming your own "bank." If you are not in that family, you are almost certain to become its victim. If you fail to accomplish this, the Sirens will seduce you repeatedly, follow you through bankruptcy, and even seduce you afterwards — incessantly, until you either die or give up.

Becoming your own "bank" is not as overwhelming a task as it might seem at first. Becoming your own "bank" is a process that involves reducing your debt-to-others and concurrently replacing it with debt to yourself. Most who undertake this effort are surprised at how quickly and efficiently they accomplish this essential transition. Much of what follows in this book helps you understand this process and make this transition.

The Venus Flytrap

A beautiful plant that is surprisingly carnivorous, the Venus Flytrap is the health care bureaucracy: doctors, hospitals, dental clinics, insurance companies, HMO's, Medicare and Medicaid, nursing homes and assisted living facilities, drug companies, and a host of other ancillary suppliers of products and services.

This Money Monster provides essential and valuable services for almost every person in our country and the world. Doctors, dentists, nurses, hospitals, insurance companies and all the other professionals who serve our medical needs contribute to our well-being. Those contributions can come from no other source. If you work directly and intimately with every sector of this bureaucracy, you will find few, if any, individuals who are not admirable in a thousand ways.

When it comes to your money, however, the Venus Flytrap can consume your wealth faster and with more aplomb than both of the other two monsters can together.

- ☞ Over 70% of all bankruptcies, 50% of foreclosures and 50% of business failures are attributable in some measure to a money drain created by health care expenses.

- ☞ Long-term care benefits through Medicaid *require* that an individual go bankrupt before they can become eligible for benefits.[6]

- ☞ If you can afford to pay for your own long-term care, it could cost you $100,000.00 per year — and the rates go up each year so by 2015 the cost may be approaching $250,000.00 per year.

- ☞ Long-term care costs at home or in a facility do not include the cost of drugs, medical care, clothing, personal care items, and other expenses that can add several more hundreds of dollars per month to the increasing cost of growing old.

- ☞ A 60-year-old self employed or unemployed individual in Colorado can pay as much as $1,000.00 a month for basic health insurance. In Florida, it is even more expensive and you do not want to know about California or New York.

- ☞ A typical transplant operation costs nearly $1,000,000.00 and that does not include the cost incurred while waiting for an organ. In addition, all of the expenses related to the procedure may not be covered by insurance.

---

6   This is not too hard apparently, since most patients who don't have long-term care insurance are broke within three months of entering a long-term care facility.

☞ A retired couple can expect to incur over $200,000.00 in un-reimbursed medical expenses during retirement.[7] That does not include home care or nursing home expenses, which currently average around $75,000.00 per year for those who need it and about $300,000.00 per couple over their lifetimes.

There are strategies and tactics that you can and must use to insulate yourself and your money from the ever-growing risk of loss due to medical expenses.

First, by becoming your own "bank" and taking advantage of Health Savings Account legislation, you can fund for much higher deductibles, significantly reduce insurance premium costs and preserve the unused money in those accounts to help cover medical expenses during retirement.

Second, you can fund comprehensive long-term care insurance through a personal "bank" and transfer the $75,000.00+ per year long-term care expense risk to an insurance company. There are two bonuses to this approach: at least a portion of the long-term care premium cost is tax deductible and, when you die, your heirs get to keep all of the money left in the "bank" you used to fund the long-term care insurance and do not have to pay any taxes on that money.

Third, a Good Attorney specializing in estate planning and taxation can show you several ways to minimize the risk to your wealth posed by this Money Monster by using trusts and other legal strategies.

---

7 Annual study conducted by Fidelity Investments.

The Behemoths

The Behemoths[8] are businesses that roam the planet enticing you to buy their products. In fact, if you buy one of those products — houses, automobiles, cereal, investments, education, mascara, iPods, computers, Xboxes, oil changes, clothing — the company selling you the product is using some of your money to promote the sale of the product to the next person and some to pay the collective finance charges that have accrued bringing the product to you.

That's not bad. It's the way economies work. What you need to be aware of is the circular and spiraling nature of the process. The seller's primary goal is not to sell you a product that makes you happy, or solves some hypothetical problem; the primary goal is to sell the next product to the next buyer — who might be you. So a portion of the money you pay for that nice new widget, is invested in an even nicer looking advertisement to entice your neighbors and friends into buying their own widgets, and ultimately to get you to upgrade or replace your widget in a couple of years.

This makes you a significant contributor to the free enterprise system. Without you and all the other contributors in the system, it simply would not work; and that's not bad either.

In fact, free enterprise is healthy. It creates competition and energizes creativity. It only becomes unhealthy for you individually when you buy products because the seller seduces you, or your social circle demands it, or you are just unaware that you are acting contrary to your own self-interest.

---

8 Behemoth is a creature mentioned in the Book of Job, 40:15-24 as the largest and most powerful animal. Metaphorically, the name has come to mean any extremely large or powerful entity.

It is unhealthy when you pay for the product multiple times by financing all or part of the purchase price through the seller or through a third party. It is unhealthy when you finance purchases, because when you do so, you allow others to control your personal economy.

Consider the discounted refrigerator you buy at the big box store using your credit card. The price of the product includes finance charges to the seller, distributor, warehouser, manufacturer, raw materials supplier, advertiser, and every other link in the chain from mining the metal to delivering the product to your door on a truck — which is also financed. When you add your credit card or commercial finance charges to the total price, you could easily wipe out the savings from any discount you received.

You cannot control what happens before you buy a product. You can control whether you buy it and how you pay for it.

Epilogue

Sometimes the word pictures we paint — Money Monsters and Behemoths that place you at risk, esoteric systems and approaches that are vague and seemingly incomprehensible — seem fuzzy and unfocused. The reality is that they are not conventional so they may seem less real.

In fact, the morbid and morose model most prevalent in America today is unreal and relies on despair. Give up...give in..."if that's all there is, my friends, then let's keep dancing."[9]

Neither hope nor hopelessness is a strategy. I believe that it is possible and necessary for you to gain control of the money that flows through your life. I know that you can master your money instead of hopelessly living as the indentured servant of the Bureaucracies and Behemoths, or hoping to marry rich or win the lottery.

There is a way. It has been tried, tested, and proven over centuries by thousands of people just like you. Some started with a fortune, some with just a little money, others with an empty purse. They all ended by passing on not just money, but more importantly, the knowledge, understanding, and wisdom needed to assure the wealth and well-being of their families for generations to come. Only you can do this for yourself, your family, and your heirs. But, you need a new model and you need a guide.

---

9   *Is that All There Is?* Peggy Lee song from the '60's.

Let this book show you the model and lead you to your guide.[10]

> "No matter how tough you think you are, you can't do this on your own..." ~ Tiger Woods

Read on...

---

10 When the term "guide" is used in this book it refers to the person or company that you rely on for financial information, advice and guidance. GUIDE is an acronym that is derived from the functions these advisors should perform on your behalf...

    G - guide and educate you to make sure you
    U - understand your personal economy and are fully
    I - informed about the products and services you
    D - decide to use in your money practices, and to
    E - escort you on your path to becoming the master of your money.

If you do not currently have a guide, or do not intend to engage one, the information in this book is comprehensive and allows you to build and manage your personal economy.

Introduction

After nearly 35 years as an insurance and financial advisor guiding others in the use of their money, I have come to realize that *most Americans are on a self-defeating path that creates wealth for governments and businesses at the expense of the well-being of individuals and families.*[11]

This is not to say that businesses are bad, or should not make money, or that government is unnecessary. America cherishes the lifestyle brought about through the efforts and innovations of its numerous large corporations, small businesses, and its exemplary form of government.

Americans have, however, individually and collectively relinquished personal freedom. They've allowed themselves to become the indentured servants of government, corporations, credit grantors, and consumer goods makers.

Over the last half century in particular, America misplaced some of its greatest treasures. These are not physical items or artifacts. They

---

11   Today's situation reminds me of the movie *Running Man,* 1987. The tagline for the movie, which depicted corporate control of the economy, entertainment and even the government to some extent, was "A game nobody survives."

are the economic principles, practices, and tools that built the most enviable economy in history.

These rock solid fundamentals, which place the value of the individual above the value of the government or of business, have been replaced by media driven drivel that seduces Americans into serving the best interest of "others" instead of doing what is best for the wealth and well-being of themselves and their families.

We call this distorted view of the economic world The Debt Paradigm. It rests on the premise that the only way to have everything you need and anything you want is with debt-to-others.

The idea that debt-to-others is not in your best interest isn't news. Two hundred years ago, Benjamin Franklin wrote in *Poor Richard's Almanac*, "But, ah! Think what you do when you run into debt; you give to another power over your liberty."

That's why I'm embracing the challenging mission of re-introducing a failsafe way for you to have the things you need and want without incurring debt-to-others; the challenging mission of re-educating Americans about money. This mission is divided into two parts.

PART I — **Change Your Mind About Money** unearths the false premises upon which current paradigm rests. It uncovers lost truths and illustrates innovative 21st century thinking about how you can use money to best serve yourself and your family. PART I also sets out clear and compelling arguments to support the approach to money described in this book.

PART II — **The Money for Life Model** describes the alternative to The Debt Paradigm in detail. The purveyors of this failed paradigm have convinced Americans that the money model that serves you best is theirs — Earn/Borrow then Spend/Repay. The Debt Paradigm creates wealth for those who manufacture, finance and sell the products you buy — at your expense.

The *Money for Life* Model, which harkens back to the financial principles upon which America was founded and incorporates 21st century thinking about money, teaches you to Earn/Save then Borrow from savings and Repay yourself.

This is not as daunting a task as it might seem at first glance. In fact, it can be accomplished by almost anyone who grasps that this approach lets YouBeTheBank; that it lets you use your money but not lose your money to the Behemoths and Bureaucracies. Many Americans today successfully employ these practices. You can too.

Many other Americans have succumbed to the seductions of advertisers and marketers of The Debt Paradigm; they have lost sight of their own best interests. If you fall into this category, I hope this book points you toward a path that better serves you, your family, and your financial future. If you have escaped from the clutches of The Debt Paradigm, you can still learn from the collected wisdom and innovative thinking found in the following pages and perhaps pass the book on to someone you know who needs it.

> "To laugh often and much; to win the respect of intelligent people and the affection of children...to leave the world a better place... to know even one life has breathed easier because you have lived. This is to have succeeded." ~ Ralph Waldo Emerson

Help me succeed. Breathe easier.

Read on...

YouBeTheBank.com

Part 1
Change Your Mind
About Money

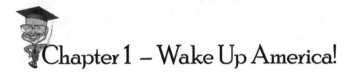# Chapter 1 – Wake Up America!

Can You "Buy" Your Way to Wealth?

> "Many a man thinks he is buying pleasure, when he is really selling himself to it." ~ Benjamin Franklin

H ave you been taught that buying is the path to wealth?

- ☞ "Buy" real estate — including your home?
- ☞ "Buy" cars or furniture or jewelry?
- ☞ "Buy" stocks and bonds?
- ☞ "Buy" computers, TV's, etc.?
- ☞ "Buy" mutual funds?

When you "buy," you send your money on a risk-based investment journey that guarantees you nothing; you create the appearance of wealth by having things you don't actually own and owning investments you don't control.

Those who seduce you with houses, cars and consumer goods want to convince you that the debt incurred when you buy the appearance of wealth is really a stepping stone to security.

The organizations that sell financial products want you to believe they have found the secret road to wealth, that theirs is the truest and surest path to financial independence, and that the risk they want you to take may not be risk at all.

I've stated the myth, but it's not the reality.

The reality is that wealth derives from *saving money* from your income and *investing* from your assets.

The Debt Paradigm teaches you something quite different. It entices you to invest from income and even to use income not yet earned — money borrowed against assets like home equity — to build your financial foundation. This is a subtle strategy that weakens the dam that retains your money and washes your wealth downstream to the collection basins of the Behemoths and Bureaucracies.

Consider that the typical family has two cars, both cars are financed or leased (another form of financing), they swim in credit card debt, and perhaps home equity debt. They also have a mortgage. All told, that typical family spends about 35% of its income paying interest to credit grantors. At the same time, they are contributing less than 5% of their income to their retirement plans and they've put much, if not all, of that retirement money at risk.

In other words, they are spending a lot more on interest than they are saving or could possibly earn from their current combined investments and savings — which are at or near zero. They cannot expect this formula to produce the results they aim to achieve.

Add to this the generally unspoken fact that being in the "stock market is like playing chicken with a freight train...no matter how many times you win, you only get to lose once."[12]   Moreover, if you have debt-to-others for consumer goods purchases when the freight train arrives, you are doubly doomed.

Greg Moore addressed the reality of debt-to-others in his 3/7/2007 DebtIntoWealth newsletter: "If you've been on planet earth over the past week, [*or any week in late July or early August 2007*] you've noticed stock markets around the globe putting on their always untimely *vanishing wealth act*. It's never a good time to lose money, and losing it in the stock market presents enormous challenges."[13]

Another myth that some Behemoths want you to believe is that you can borrow money to buy the products they recommend without damaging your finances. They don't tell you that when you borrow, you risk your money *twice*—once in the debt and again in the purchase. They don't emphasize that, when you move money that you control

---

12   Stated by Mike Masters, profiled in "Stock Market Wizards: Interviews with America's Top Stock Traders" by Jack D Schwager — 2003 — pp 206-221

13   Greg Moore, DebtIntoWealth.com newsletter 3/7/2007 (italics added) The newsletter goes on to clarify: "Suppose you're fortunate enough to make a 20% return and suppose you're also unfortunate enough to get handed a 20% loss. What's your average percent gain? Well... (+20 plus -20 is 0) divided by 2 is 0%. You have a 0% average return... but... did you lose money? Yup. And it doesn't matter which order the gains or losses occurred. For example, suppose you start with $1000. If it grows by 20%, you now have $1200. If $1200 now falls by 20%, you're left with $960. Do this math the other way, with the loss occurring first, and you're left with this same $960.

»   "Even though your returns averaged 0%, you lost money! *Stock market investing by its very nature creates gains and losses.* In order to make money, your gains must overcome losses plus taxes, plus fees, plus f.

»   "*Unless you're very, very good...and lucky...you're probably better off pursuing less risky wealth building strategies.* Yes. I'm aware of historical averages. I'm also aware that it's mathematically impossible for the average investor to achieve them. Why? Because historical averages don't pay taxes or fees, aren't adjusted for inflation, and aren't trapped by untimely vanishing wealth..."

or the equity from your home into one of their products, you weaken your own money foundation.

Remember, "investments" and material possessions are not "money." Only money is money. However, the people who sell investments and consumer goods don't get paid in kind. They earn some of *your money* every time you buy from them—whether or not that's a good idea for you.[14]

The sellers of investments don't tell you that only the top few percent of the population has enough assets to assume the risk of loss inherent in many of the risk-based products they sell.[15] Indeed, they gloss over this fact: Over 90% of the people who "retire" have a significantly reduced lifestyle because they believed they could buy wealth during their working years. After retiring, they found out that the strategy didn't work the way they thought it would. The jewelry, furniture, cars and appliances they bought are worthless and the income they need is missing in action.

Consider these comments from a Wall Street watchdog:

> "In planning, forget assets, focus on income. The fallacy with Wall Street's logic is...simple: They focus on assets, the exact same strategy Goldman-Sachs, Merrill Lynch, and Wall Street's insiders have been focusing on since the mid–1990s. Why? Because it's making billions. *Between 1995 and 2005 this strategy has roughly tripled assets under management for Wall Street and*

---

14 "Trying to beat the stock market is theoretically a zero-sum game (for every winner, there must be a loser), but after the substantial costs of investing are deducted, it becomes a loser's game."... Jack Bogle, the Bogle Research Institute, June 2007.

15 Remember Dr Agon Fly's rule that one should save from income and invest from assets.

mutual fund firms, according to Jack Bogle, the Bogle Research Institute, [June 2007] *with annual revenues also tripling to over $350 billion by 2005, while returns to Main Street investors have actually declined in the past decade."* [16]

"Through want of enterprise and faith men are where they are, buying and selling and spending their lives like servants." ~ Henry David Thoreau

Read on...

---

16   Thursday, March 08, 2007 By Paul B. Farrell. © 2006 MarketWatch, Inc.

A New Way to Master Your Spending

> "Live within your means, never be in debt, and by husbanding your money you can always lay it out well. But when you get in debt you become a slave. Therefore I say to you never involve yourself in debt, and become no man's surety." ~ Andrew Jackson

I suggest you consider setting up a new foundation and framework for managing your money before you decide to use it to buy wealth; that you gain a clear perspective and adopt a tested system that helps you master—on an ongoing, long-term basis—your everyday spending.

Start by addressing the spending you do that typically incurs debt, including:

- ☞ purchase of a home
- ☞ buying autos
- ☞ paying interest on credit cards
- ☞ using store charge cards
- ☞ paying for education — from pre-school on
- ☞ buying furniture, appliances, recreational vehicles
- ☞ taking vacations
- ☞ covering the cost of children's weddings
- ☞ making home repairs and additions
- ☞ indulging in: smoking, gambling, alcohol, shopping, make your own list
- ☞ dealing with the unexpected:
  - medical expenses for: you, your spouse, your children, your parents,
  - loss of health insurance
  - loss of income: disability, unemployment, divorce, care for aging parents, legal problems, identity theft, dishonest friends or employees
  - children gone astray: drugs, alcohol, sex, gambling.

You also need a clear idea about how you'll pay your way for the next 30 to 70 years. That's right. If you're a healthy 65 year-old, you may have 30 or more years to live. If you are 30 and take good care of yourself, you can count on living to age 100 or beyond.

> "Americans no longer look to government for economic security..."
> ~ Bill Owens, former governor of Colorado

So, other than Social Security, which many economists, investment analysts and everyday Americans see as a failed system that is doomed, you need to have money that will guarantee you the following:

- ☞ income that adjusts with inflation and pays for
  - housing, cars, food, clothing
  - travel, entertainment, leisure activities like tennis, golf, skiing, etc.
  - gifts for children, grandchildren, great grandchildren
  - all the items you spend money on today
- ☞ money to deal with unexpected expenses
- ☞ money for steadily increasing medical care costs and for long-term care expenses that can run into 6 figures annually and could exceed $250,000 a year by 2015 (studies show that one of every two Americans will probably need care either at home or in a facility for up to 20 years)
- ☞ a legacy that encapsulates your wisdom with the money you leave behind for future generations

What long and daunting lists! And they're not comprehensive. Yet every single item, and many more, needs your rapt and continuing attention.

Read on ...

What the Behemoths Do

Do you think the Behemoths that want you to buy their products and put your money in the investments they recommend (which means you put *your money* at risk, not theirs) can guarantee you'll have your money when you need it most: when you're 97 and feeble, 77 and suffering with Alzheimer's, 57 and disabled in a sporting accident, or 37 in your prime and dealing with MS?

No! We all know that the consumer products we buy offer no long term value and that the companies that sell risk-based products are not even *allowed* to say the word "guarantee."

The sellers of investments can't make a promise or even imply that the money you invest with them won't be decimated by a depression or ravaged by a recession. They can't assure you that you'll have even one cent in your account when you need it most.

Remember in 2002 when almost 80% of those who planned to retire decided to work another 5 to 10 years? They realized they had to recover the loss they suffered after the recession, which began in 1999 and was worsened by the events on 9/11/2001? Those who sell investments, however, still got paid for leading Americans on a fool's journey and didn't automatically suffer the losses that their clients did.[17]

---

17   For a scathing indictment of the investment-behemoths refer to *Wall Street Versus America: The Rampant Greed and Dishonesty That Imperil Your Investments*, by Gary Weiss, Portfolio, 290 pages.

A Place for Independent Planners

In case it seems like I'm being too harsh with those who sell invest-ments, let me add this perspective. There is a very definite place for investing and for using the services of an *independent* investment ad-visor, especially an *independent* Certified Financial Planning Practi-tioner®. Whether your planner is commission-based, fee-based or a hybrid of the two, your planner offers critical guidance as you master your money. I personally would not consider making investment deci-sions without the advice of my personal Certified Financial Planning Practitioner®.[18]

The role of investment advisors should be well defined, just as the roles of bankers, insurance agents, mortgage brokers, attorneys, and CPA's are clearly defined. Many of these advisors play an essential role on your team and act honestly and effectively as your guides. Others fit the old adage that "If the only tool you have is a hammer, everything looks like a nail," leading you on the only path they know and not where you want or need to go.[19]

What's the most important consideration when deciding what to do about money—including investing and choosing an investment advi-sor? It is this: that *you* maintain control of all of the money that flows through your life; that *you* choose when to use money to support your financial foundation and framework and *when* it makes sense to you to put some (never all) of *your money* at risk.

---

18   I want to clarify that I am not recommending that you buy investments without first putting a financial foundation and framework in place.

19   "[Captive] Advisers often wind up selling the proprietary products [of their com-panies], because they flock like moths to a flame to products paying greater compensa-tion," said Andrew Stoltmann, a securities attorney and partner with Stoltmann Law Offices PC in Chicago.

Let's review some of the points I've made so far:

- ☞ Control the money that flows through your life.
- ☞ Change your paradigm. Adopt the principles and practices found in this book and establish a solid foundation and strong framework for managing money and creating wealth.
- ☞ Financial planners, bankers and any other "expert guides" you might hire need to recognize and respect that you are the *master of your money* — not them.

"Sudden power is apt to be insolent, sudden liberty saucy; that behaves best which has grown gradually." ~ Benjamin Franklin

Read on…

Shake Up the Current Paradigm

"The truth you believe and cling to makes you unavailable to hear anything new." ~ Pema Chödrön, Buddhist Monk, author and teacher

A paradigm is an internal model of something. In this book, paradigm refers to the economic model you use to justify your decisions about money. Your paradigm can have positive or negative effects. If you are like most who have read this far, you probably know already that you need to think about changing something in your decision making process.

Paradigms are subtle. They lurk in the darker recesses of your psyche and the labyrinth of your mind. They manifest in every act of every day without asking your permission or identifying themselves.

Have you ever had this experience? A person tells you something that is indisputably true, but that contradicts one of your long-standing beliefs. You recoil and protest that it can't be true. That's your paradigm speaking.

Here's an example. A friend calls you on a bright September morning and tells you that two jumbo jets have just flown into the Twin Towers in New York. "What?" you exclaim. "That's nuts. This is America. People don't do that here. You gotta be kidding. Is it on the news? Oh my God! It's true. Who could do such a thing?"

The paradigm—that you were safe from terror in America—reluctantly climbed out of its cave on 9/11/2001 and, in just a few short hours, collapsed as the Twin Towers came down.

This initial shocking event is only the beginning of the process, however. To fully divest yourself of the paradigm requires a conscious decision to dispense with it, and a subsequent decision to replace it with a more effective model — in this example, one that accepts the possibility of foreign terror on American soil. To do otherwise in the face of the failure of the old paradigm is to simply wait for it to fail again.

When it comes to your money paradigm, use this book to help you mine the caverns of your mind and probe the recesses of your psyche to discover—and then redefine—the misconceptions hiding there. As Dr. Zink implied in the Foreward, the more aware you become, the more control you exercise over your money and the more control you have over your life.

When America was founded over 200 years ago, "Americans were better at producing (wealth) than most other people...the farmers, merchants, manufacturers, and artisans whose interactions with the financial system, and with the governmental institutions and policies that supported that system, insured that the economy remained highly meritocratic, that it dispersed its fruits fairly, if not evenly."[20] The paradigm that supported this system relied on an individual's freedom to choose a path and follow it to success — or failure. In the past 35 years this paradigm has been tweaked and twisted so much that, today, it's a Frankenstein's monster that has seized control of America's money.

> "It's time to regain control of your money — and your life." ~ Dr Agon Fly

No doubt you have a unique paradigm driving your behavior regarding money. And you likely share some of the prejudices and assumptions

---

20   Wright, Robert E., and Cohen, David J., Financial Founding Fathers. University of Chicago Press. 2006. p1.

of the dysfunctional paradigm prevalent in our society and economy today. That's why I encourage you to probe the depths of your own mind and psyche to discover your money paradigm. What prejudices do you bring to the decisions you make about your money and finances?

On a larger scale, I want to expose the deep-seated social and cultural programming that reinforces—through consumer product advertising, financial product design, and financial advisor training (delivered mostly by the Behemoths that sell investments)—the flawed paradigm that dominates thinking in America today, at the beginning of the 21st century.

Read on...

The Proof is in Performance

> "Credit leads into a desert with invisible boundaries." ~ Anton Chekhov

How flawed is today's paradigm? Here are a few facts and observations that will get you started on the path of discovery. [21] [*Dr Agon Fly's comments in brackets*]

☞ There were 1.3 billion credit cards in circulation in the U.S. in 2004. The top 10 credit card issuers controlled 86% of the general-purpose credit card market share in 2005, up from 55% ten years earlier. [*Gee! I wonder if they are motivated by your best interest or theirs; 86% gets close to a monopoly, Hmmm! I wonder who lobbied hardest for the restructuring of the bankruptcy laws in 2003–5 to assure that credit card companies would lose less money when someone they seduced (like you or me) loses everything.*]

☞ The credit card industry took in $43 billion in fee income from late payments, over-limits, and balance transfer fees in 2004, up from $39 billion in 2003. [*Wow! All that at $29.00 a shot ($39.00 in 2007). Go figure—the banks certainly do.*]

American Consumer Debt

☞ Total American consumer debt reached $2.2 trillion in 2005. [*And that doesn't count the federal government's debt of—who knows how many trillions!*]

☞ Total American consumer debt first reached $1 trillion in 1994. [*Double your money, double your fun.*]

---

21 Statistics and information from CreditCard.com, December 2006.

☞ Total American household consumer debt averaged $11,840 in 2005. [*Are you falling behind? Go. Quickly! Buy something on credit.*]

☞ Total American consumer debt increased 41% between 1998 and 2004. [*Pretty steep growth curve. Oops! in the wrong direction for you, but not for the Behemoths.*]

☞ The average amount financed for new car purchases was just over $26,000 in 2005. [*My parents purchased their home for $12,000 in 1954.*]

☞ Average household credit card debt has increased 167% between 1990 and 2004. [*Pretty steep growth curve; Oops! in the wrong direction — again.*]

☞ The average interest rate paid on credit cards was approximately 14.54% in 2005. [*Do you know the top rate a credit card company can charge you? There is no "top rate." They can charge you as much as they want. I recently saw one at over 54%.*]

☞ In 2005, the rate of personal savings in the United States dipped below 0% for the first time since the great depression (1932–33), hitting -.5%. It dropped to -.01% in 2006. [*Scary, isn't it! The general economy is booming, while personal economies crash and burn.*]

☞ Approximately 96% of Americans will have to retire financially dependent on the government, family, or charity, according to a 2003 study. [*I can hardly wait...won't it be great!*]

☞ A typical credit card purchase costs 12%-18% more than if cash is used (as of 2004). [*Imagine what that adds up to in a few years.*]

☞ As of 2004, 23% of Americans admitted to maxing out a credit card. [*I wonder how many didn't admit it.*]

☞ 2.39 million U.S. households filed for bankruptcy in 2005, a 12.8% increase over 2004. [*That was before the credit-card-company-rescue legislation by our, admittedly, not-too-smart and lobbyist-driven Congress.*]

☞ The average credit card balance in 2005 would require over 13 years to pay off if only making minimum payments of 4% at an average interest rate of 14% [*and that's probably more than 24 years at 18%*]. [22]

☞ 5% of Americans used a credit card to make their tax payment in 2004 [*and I'm guessing that was not just for convenience*].

☞ 30 million Americans (40% of homeowners) refinanced their mortgages during the 3 years prior to Q3 2005, with over half applying the proceeds to eliminate credit card debt [*and someone, we won't mention names, said that was a good idea, then got paid for it*].

☞ Among middle-class households, the average amount of credit card debt paid off with home equity loans was $12,000 (Q3 2005). [*You'll meet Stanley "up to my eyeballs in debt" Johnson, the poster child for home refinancing, a bit later.*]

☞ Seven out of 10 [over 70%] low-income and middle-income households reported using their credit cards as a financial safety net, i.e., to pay for car repairs, rent or housing repairs and medical expenses, rather than relying on savings in 2005. [*I'd guess not having any savings might account for that.*]

---

22 In 2001, Wesley Wannemacher charged $3,200 on his [credit] card to pay for his wedding. During the next six years, he paid $4,900 in interest charges, $1,500 in over-the-limit charges, and $1,100 in late fees for a total of $10,700. As of last month, he still owed $4,400 on the card. — reported on Yahoo Financial, "Congress Takes On Credit Cards," by Brian Wingfield. 03/07/07.

☞ According to a 2004 study, the number one cause of divorce is financial stress. [*Is this the road you want to travel? Ask your children.*]

Especially for Seniors

"You can be young without money but you can't be old without it."
~ Tennessee Williams

☞ In 2004, the average debt for Americans [aged] 65 and older was $4,000, up 89% in the past decade [*and remember, older folks tend to be secretive about their finances... the true number is probably a lot higher.*}

☞ In 2004, the average personal wealth of a 50-year-old American was less than $40,000 including home equity. [*That's pitiful after working 30 years or so.*]

☞ In 2004, most credit card debt of older Americans was driven by healthcare expenses and the increased cost of prescription medication. [*And none of the Bureaucracies or Behemoths told them that they would have to face this dilemma.*]

What is the big picture these bits and pieces of information paint?

It's the picture of a failed paradigm.

Therefore, it's imperative that you ask these questions:

1. Does the paradigm reflected in these statistics and observations reflect the values that built America into the most robust and imitated economy in the world?

2. Is it the cultural and societal paradigm that you want to use when you make decisions about money?

3. Is the reality of the senior citizens' experiences what you want for yourself as you age and for your parents as they grow older?

Wouldn't you want to run from this paradigm like a gazelle being chased by a cheetah?

Start running. That's the current paradigm and the cheetah is on the prowl.

Read on...

Where Do You Go From Here?

> "Nothing will ever be attempted, if all possible objections must first be overcome." ~ Samuel Johnson

Where should you go? What should you do?

The Behemoths that design and promote the current paradigm sell you the products — both consumer products and investment products — that will make *them* wealthy. They are *not committed* to *your* growth and security but to their own. So, where can you go to find a model that serves you?

Discover an old paradigm made new by the failure of the current paradigm to help individuals and families.

Learn how to lay a foundation that lets you control the money that flows through your life and lets you employ that money to:

- ☞ Live free from debt-to-others

- ☞ Create income you don't have to work for and that you can't outlive

- ☞ Make sure you have money when you need it because a life event like job loss, accidents, divorce, disease or any of a thousand other life events causes a loss of income or unexpected expenses

- ☞ Assure that you can *pay forward* your wealth and wisdom to your children, grandchildren, and every generation that follows you as long as America stands as the beacon of freedom and free enterprise that the world has looked to for leadership for the past two centuries.

When you do this, you will be the *master of your money*. You will, by gaining control of your *personal* economy and teaching your children how to do the same, help other Americans regain control of their personal economies. Most importantly, you will help America recapture the economic and financial values that have been tossed in a dumpster in exchange for "having stuff" that you don't own and owning investments you don't control.

Read on…

Exercises in Money Awareness

"Be industrious and frugal, and you will be rich." ~ Benjamin Franklin

Every age has its money paradigm and every paradigm has its foundations in the thinking of those who, like Benjamin Franklin, are influential enough to affect the society in which they live.

The basic American money paradigm that built the greatest national economy in recorded history still reverberates within the caverns of the American psyche. Often, however, its echoes are only background noise amid the cacophony of the many and often conflicting TV, radio, internet, print and other media messages — the siren songs — that bombard our consciousness every hour of every day.

Remember, too, that the Behemoths and Bureaucracies employ millions of individual sales and marketing reps to reinforce, during one-on-one meetings, their messages to consumers like you and me.

Your first assignment, therefore — if you want to escape from this incoherent maze of messages about money — is to step back and look carefully at your own paradigm.

- ☞ Is it a subset of the current failed model?

- ☞ Does it contain elements from the thinking of the founders of America's money model?

- ☞ Do you have your own preconceptions that irrationally rule your money practices?

In the next few pages you will have the opportunity to pause briefly and consider these and other questions surrounding money. The goal of this opening chapter is to allow you to consider your starting point when it comes to money. You do not have to draw any conclusions; just permit yourself to recognize some of the elements that support and perpetuate your personal money paradigm.

Read on...

Becoming Aware of the Money in Your Life

> "It is challenging to face the "dark side" of how you handle money — or the doubts, fears, worries, and thwarted hopes that may appear. Sometimes it's hard to see the hidden treasure, but when we tell the truth about what we see, even when we don't want to see it, we're given even more strength." ~ Maria Nemeth, Ph.D., *The Energy of Money*

Explore the labyrinths of your mind. Try to uncover as many of the shibboleths[23] as possible that are hiding there or cowering in some crevasse in your psyche. Seriously question what you feel about these preconceived notions about money. Not every idea you discover will be a shibboleth. Some of them may be healthy and useful, but most will be the result of years and years of ingesting the flawed reasoning of the Debt Paradigm that was fed to you, without truly questioning any of its base assumptions.

Subsequent chapters in this book will address many issues surrounding the current paradigm, but for now just write down your thoughts and feelings so you can compare and contrast them with the conclusions you draw later on.

---

23   A shibboleth is a saying or idea that one holds to be true just because it's been held so by many others for some period of time. In 1492 the flatness of the earth was a shibboleth.

What's important about money to you?

> "Money is like fire, an element as little troubled by moralizing as earth, air and water. Men can employ it as a tool or they can dance around it as if it were the incarnation of a god. Money votes socialist or monarchist, finds a profit in pornography or translations from the Bible, commissions Rembrandt and underwrites the technology of Auschwitz. It acquires its meaning from the uses to which it is put." ~ Lewis H. Lapham

The words and ideas that leap into the forefront of your consciousness when you consider this question are most likely conventional wisdom,[24] the shibboleths that scramble out of their caverns on cue whenever a discussion of money begins.

The answers that are truly meaningful to you are the answers that you discover when you probe more deeply into your feelings and thinking; when you begin to recognize that the worn out clichés that jump up and demand to be heard are shallow, and empty of personal meaning. They are the ideas and words of the Bureaucracies and Behemoths and not the ideas that spring from your heart or from personal evaluation.

Write your thoughts and insights. Identify them as "Conventional Wisdom", meaning they belong to someone else, or "MINE"...belonging to you.

---

24 My definition of "conventional wisdom" is doing what everyone else does and thinking what everyone else thinks because that is what they do and that is what they think.

Do you have a clear vision when it comes to your relationship with money?

> "Though no one can go back and make a brand new start, anyone can start from now and make a brand new ending." ~ Carl Bard

Having a "clear vision" is the logical successor to the previous question. Are you seriously considering your relationship with money in real terms — in terms of yourself and your financial future? You can decide what "destination" means to you. What it means in the context of this book will develop as you progress through the pages.

Be aware, however, that this is not a goal setting exercise. It is not important to decide what you want to achieve with money. This exercise is about how you want to relate to money.

The question is a bit vague but the more specific your answers, the better they will serve you as you learn to *master your money*.

Do you have a simple and accurate way to measure yourself when it comes to money?

"If you don't know where you're going, any road will get you there."
~ Lewis Carroll, Alice in Wonderland

Once you have a clearer vision of how you want to relate to money, you need to discover a path that allows you to actualize that vision. That means you have to have a way to measure your progress.

Sometimes this exercise leads to simplistic answers such as "Save 10%," use a budget, or "Max out my 401(k)," as opposed to discovering any clear and accurate measuring devices. Don't be too concerned about that now. The end product of this exercise is not to actually devise a measuring system but to become aware of the ideas implanted by The Debt Paradigm that you carry around with you that pass as measuring tools but don't serve very well.

Write what flows naturally and *beware the shibboleths*. As you progress through this book you will discover easy to use gauges for measuring your progress with money.

Are you Master of Your Money?

> "There are no secrets to success. It is the result of preparation, hard work, learning from failure." ~ General Colin Powell

Are you in charge of your money? What is your discretionary income each month — the money you actually control after fixed, necessary expenses? And remember, any expense you are unwilling to give up unless forced to, like the expensive car, or the daily latte, is fixed. Your cable bill is not strictly necessary, but if you're not going to cancel it, it's fixed.

Are you spending everything you earn or more? What is your true net worth? Make a list:

☞ what you own

☞ what you owe

☞ what you earn, and

☞ where it goes.

Be thoughtful and thorough — stern and honest.

Don't list things in "what you own" like your furniture or personal items that you'd be lucky to sell for ten cents on the dollar. You are not applying for a loan or anticipating an insurance claim. This exercise is for you.

One measure of your real net-worth in the number of months you can survive without an income and without invading your investments.[25] Be careful also to consider the simple non-essentials of daily life such as a latte` or a movie now and then when you are deciding what your basic monthly needs are. It's simply bad planning to expect to live without an occasional break from austerity. Appendix B has additional guidelines and tools to help you.

Looking Forward...

In the following pages, you will discover what it means to become the Master of Your Money...

☞ You'll find a starting point and see a destination...

☞ You'll learn the secrets that make the wealthy — you know, wealthy — and keep them that way...

☞ You'll find out that you can measure and manage your money
   a. with simple recordkeeping
   b. without complex charts, graphs, spreadsheets
   c. without the risk that is inherent in many financial plans and products

☞ *And most importantly, you'll realize that money is more than currency; it is a medium of communication that directly reflects your values.*

Read on...

---

25   Conventional wisdom tells you that you need 3 to 6 months ready cash to allow for emergencies. I believe that 3 to 5 years is more realistic. You'll see examples later in the book that support this idea.

Chapter 2 – What is an Economy?

" 'Money talks' because money is a metaphor, a transfer, and a bridge. Like words and language, money is a storehouse of communally achieved work, skill, and experience. Money, however, is also a specialist technology like writing; and as writing intensifies the visual aspect of speech and order, and as the clock visually separates time from space, so money separates work from the other social functions. Even today money is a language for translating the work of the farmer into the work of the barber, doctor, engineer, or plumber. As a vast social metaphor, bridge, or translator, money—like writing—speeds up exchange and tightens the bonds of interdependence in any community. It gives great spatial expansion and control to political organizations, just as writing does, or the calendar. " ~ Marshall McLuhan

ENCARTA, the online dictionary, defines "Economy" this way:

Economy: The production and consumption of goods and services of a community, regarded as a whole.

The Oxford dictionary adds another perspective:

Economy: The wealth and resources of a community, especially in terms of the production and consumption of goods and services.

We all understand "production and consumption" — the common factor in both definitions. We all produce and we all consume. The generally accepted role for individuals and families is, however, consumption. In fact, the pundits and bureaucrats do not see us as individuals. To the theorists we are consumers. As individuals we produce nothing when it comes to economic theory and reporting. The companies we work for produce and we may contribute to that productivity, but when it comes to reporting our participation in the economy, we consume. That is our perceived value in the economic community.

What about the rest of the Encarta definition: "A community regarded as a whole..." Are we not a part of that community? Well, of course we are and our role as consumers is defined at the macro level. On the other hand, which economy are we talking about: the world economy? The US economy? The economy of your state; your city; your school system; your homeowners association; your church, synagogue or mosque? How about your own individual economy and your family's economy? Is there not the production and consumption of goods and services involved at your house too?

The Oxford dictionary helps answer these questions and leads us to what we're really after here: a working definition of personal economy. The Oxford definition adds "wealth and resources" to the equation, allowing us to connect our own situations to those of the "community as a whole" from the Encarta definition. For our purposes, the main component of "wealth and resources" for an individual or family is money.

Therefore, a definition of a personal economy that works well for this book is this:

The production of money by a family or individual in order to create the personal wealth and resources needed to acquire goods and services and secure their future.

It would be great if that definition were perfectly clear all by itself. I want to elaborate on it, however, to make sure it relates accurately to the rest of the ideas we are going to share.

While businesses and broader economies produce "goods and services" you and your families (apart from your businesses if you are employers or self-employed) produce money. The money that you produce is the raw material from which you create your personal wealth.

Your personal wealth is the resource you employ to create your environment — your home, furniture, cars, clothing, etc. — and the lifestyle you desire. This environment is both the product and the basis of your personal economy.

There are two components of these equations and definitions you should keep in mind:

First, production comes before consumption. This is obvious when you read it. It is not as obvious in the behavior of the general population.

The Government Accounting Office reported recently that:

> "…financial literacy is appallingly poor. A growing body of evidence indicates that many Americans are lacking in financial literacy. Numerous studies have shown most adults have not mastered *basic economic concepts*…" [Emphasis added.][26]

Remember, also, the facts and statistics about debt recounted in Chapter 1. How many people have incurred mortgages beyond their ability to repay? The turmoil in the financial markets beginning in mid-2007 and continuing as we write [December, 2007] is directly related to sub-prime[27] lending practices. I heard a story recently about a retired person who was sold a mortgage with a $1,100.00 per month payment, and he had only a $1,200.00 per month income.

A friendly acquaintance of mine told me he had bought a work truck for his business for $4,000.00 *over* sticker price because the truck he was trading in on the new vehicle was worth thousands of dollars less than the amount he owed on it. It took him nearly seven years to climb out of that debtor's ditch.

These people put the cart of consumption (a shopping cart, perhaps) before the horse of production.

> A second and equally significant idea in the Personal Economy definition is that you use your money to create a lifestyle for yourself and for your family. This too may seem obvious, but when you look critically at where your money goes, and who is getting rich from that money, you may begin to change your perspective.

---

26 The Government Accounting Office, Financial Literacy and Education Commission, Further Progress Needed to Ensure In Effective National Strategy, GAO-07-100, p1.

27 In the simplest of terms "sub-prime" refers to loans that are made to individuals with weaker credit who may not be fully qualified to borrow.

Every item you purchase — gasoline, candy bars, mutual funds, your 401(k), auto insurance, a house, a mortgage — makes some other person, government taxing authority or company richer.

Every time you purchase a product or investment using credit, it makes at least two others richer — the producer and the credit granting company. *No purchase ever makes you richer.* Every time you buy, it adds to someone else's wealth.

If you are lucky and wise, your purchase may fetch a price higher than you paid if you sell it at some future date. The purchase itself, however, didn't put money in your pocket. It did put money into someone else's wallet.

Again, this is not necessarily a bad thing. Free enterprise works well. Without it, you could not purchase anything. We are describing the reality that confronts us. We are not judging it as good or bad (although I have yet to find an alternative better than free enterprise.) Your role is not to rant against the system or demean those who are successful using it. Your aim should be to gain a deeper understanding of how the system works — *to change your perspectives and your paradigm* — and then to use the system, not to the detriment of others but for your own and your family's benefit.

Here's what's important:

- ☞ Change your perspective — your paradigm
- ☞ You already have a personal economy
- ☞ Production must precede consumption or financial failure is almost certain
- ☞ Who do you want to make wealthy?
  - • Put your savings first, your lifestyle second, your investment (risk) la r and wealth is the result.
  - • No purchase, including an investment, can promise to make you richer but your purchases always put money into someone else's pocket

Read on…

Chapter 3 – The Debt Paradigm

> "Money is a singular thing. It ranks with love as man's greatest source of joy. And with death as his greatest source of anxiety. Over all history it has oppressed nearly all people in one of two ways: either it has been abundant and very unreliable, or reliable and very scarce." ~ John Kenneth Galbraith

A Little Bit of History

E conomic paradigms are not modern phenomena. A prevailing economic paradigm always surfaces when one analyzes the character of the country and the world. The following discussion is a simple account of the various paradigms that have broadly prevailed in America since its founding.[28]

---

28   Historians, please forgive the license I take in reducing something as complex as economic history to a few short and oversimplified eras. My undergraduate degree in History taught me that one could never force a few hundred years and a few million people into a single book, much less a few paragraphs, so I claim no historical credits. This stratagem is solely to create a context for the ideas in this and subsequent chapters.

The Founders Paradigm

The concepts and practices found in this book were as fundamental to the thinking of most of the Founding Fathers as were the structure of government defined by the Constitution and the Bill of Rights. One needs only read Benjamin Franklin's *The Way to Wealth* to discover the genesis of much of the thinking of the time. The First Bank of North America and the First and Second Banks of the United States embodied the principles that have helped guide America to its place of pre-eminence in the world today.

During the Colonial and Revolutionary periods of our history, it was the strong banking and financial leaders in America that established her as a power to be reckoned with and as an economic and trading partner, which Europe (the economic center of the world at the time) could rely on. Were it not for a few brave and bright men, the Republicans of the day would have eliminated the banking system altogether and allowed America to once again become the servant of greedy, contentious, and disorganized European powers.[29]

The Founders' Paradigm found its voice in Alexander Hamilton and its ultimate opponent in President Andrew Jackson. Jackson fought and won a battle to prevent the Bank of the United States from renewing its charter, and plunged the nation into a severe recession that lasted for nearly a decade (1837 – 1843). Fortunately, the American people that Jackson honestly thought he was helping

---

29   The Republicans of the colonial and constitutional era, (called Democrats or liberals today) led by Thomas Jefferson, opposed any kind of central banking system and many, especially the New England contingent, would have happily returned our fledgling nation to British rule — and almost did. Had Jefferson's decimation of the army and attempts to destroy the banking system prevailed, America would have lost the War of 1812 and returned to British rule. For a thorough discussion of the financial world of early America ref Wright, Robert E., and Cohen, David J., Financial Founding Fathers. University of Chicago Press. 2006.

were able to survive his ill-advised economic surgery and move westward.

The Frontier Paradigm

Between the depression induced by Jackson's de-authorization of the central banking system and the Civil War, the national economy grew, based on a foundation of westward expansion and the stabilization of businesses in the eastern part of the country. The people of that time believed in the promise America held for all individuals to build a solid future for themselves and their families. What I call the Frontier Paradigm was a reflection of that belief.

Much of the economy relied on agrarian businesses in the south and west as both consumers and producers of goods. Most invention and manufacturing aimed at serving these businesses and supporting international trade was located in the East. Although there were pockets of consumer-oriented manufacturing and sales — the general store in the countryside and on the Main Streets of small towns, the department stores in the cities — most industry aimed to supply the farmers, ranchers, settlers and traders who were in the vanguard of America's push west. Most commerce, from shipbuilding to the nascent railroad industry, supported the westward expansion of America, or the frontier of international trade.

The Industrial Paradigm

> "There is no legislation—I care not what it is—tariff, railroads, corporations, or of a general political character, that all equals in importance the putting of our banking and currency system on the sound basis..." ~ William Howard Taft

The Civil War and the settlement of the west changed everything. The manufacturing of items that could be produced in large quantities and shipped all over the country and the world became the prevalent preoccupation of businesses. This led to the consolidation of resources, the era of monopolies and the building of great American families and fortunes.

This period also experienced the stock market crash of 1907 which gave birth to the Federal Reserve system and a new way of seeing the banking industry. During this era, the banking and investing businesses regained some of the economic and political strength and stature that had been eroded by the Jacksonian assault.

The Industrial Paradigm lasted until the conclusion of the First World War. Largely as a result of its success, Europe and much of the rest of the world witnessed the maturing of America as both an economic and a political power.

The Anything Goes Paradigm

America was euphoric after WWI. The financial outlook was rosy in most people's eyes. Industry was booming. Large corporations like E.I. DuPont were diversifying their product lines. The economic prosperity opened up cultural space in which various social movements could prosper as well. Everyone had an issue it seemed and many were competing with each other; prohibition, women's suffrage, and unbridled investing. Automobiles were becoming the ascendant form of transportation, and the airplane was beginning to impact transportation and commerce. Anything was possible and everything was tried.

This era also saw the rise of underregulated banking and unfettered financial markets. We all know what happened next. The William Cowper was precipitated by a lack of regulation in the financial markets and perpetuated by a worldwide depression which eventually led America into WWII.

The Scarcity Paradigm – Part I

From the crash of 1929 until the Second World War, America lived with ceaseless scarcity and unrelenting uncertainty. Jobs were scarce. Good jobs, even scarcer. Food was in short supply. Farmers were hardly able to produce enough food to feed their families. Businesses and entire industries were under siege and many barely survived.

> "As the economic depression deepened in the early 30s...banks began to fail at alarming rates. During the 20s, there was an average of 70 banks failing each year nationally. After the crash, during the first 10 months of 1930, 744 banks failed — 10 times as many. In all, 9,000 banks failed during the decade of the 30s. By 1933, depositors saw $140 billion disappear through bank failures." [30]

This environment taught some great lessons to Americans about thrift and the uncertainty of economic conditions: the hallmarks of the Scarcity Paradigm. The failure of so many banks, the Federal Reserve System and thousands of employers reminded Americans of the need for self-sufficiency.

---

30   http://www.livinghistoryfarm.org.

The conditions that led to these conclusions came to a clear and precipitous halt with the onset of WWII. The war reinforced who we were as Americans — our strength, our resolve, our Judeo-Christian values, and our place in the world. It did not, however, erase the lessons learned during the Great Depression.

The Scarcity Paradigm – Part II

When millions of Americans returned to some semblance of normalcy after World War II, the lessons of the depression era remained. They were fully ingrained in the paradigmatic thinking of most Americans by the tumultuous and painful events of the decade and a half from 1930 to 1945. Job security, frugality in periods of abundance, paying off the mortgage, and the nearness of death in a dangerous world - these were the cement that held the Scarcity Paradigm together.

It took eighty million babies, The Korean Conflict, the Civil Rights Movement, the Vietnam War and the men and women whose spirits permeated those turbulent years to transform the Scarcity Paradigm. The result was not, however, a clearly defined new paradigm. The Vietnam War and the post-Vietnam War era, instead, generated a multi-colored, even psychedelic economic environment.

The Psychedelic Paradigm

During the 1960s and into the 1980s America experimented with everything from drugs to government intervention in the free market system during the Nixon and Carter administrations. Some of the experiments worked and others didn't.

Interest rates soared and inflation soared even higher. Speculation on everything from real estate to valueless stocks to commodities and precious metals, made millions for the lucky few and more millions for bankruptcy attorneys who served the many.

The clear message that came out of The Psychedelic Paradigm was that managing an economy of any scale without possessing clarity and economic common sense simply would not work.

Other messages emerged also and became the basis for a more subtle but equally devastating embryonic paradigm. America fell in love with the dream of having everything they needed and anything they wanted when they needed and wanted it. Americans came to believe paradigmatically that they could spontaneously actualize this fantasy. Businesses — especially the Behemoths — encouraged this perversion of the American Dream of security and plenty.

My stepfather had three cars in his lifetime: a 1940 Chevy, a 1956 Chevy, and a 1967 Chevy. He owned one 750 square foot house where he and my mother both breathed their last breaths. He was among the Greatest Generation — the generation that held onto the Scarcity Paradigm until death.

Members of my generation (the Forgotten Generation 1924–1945), and the Boomers who followed, grew up with WWII veterans for parents and our Great Depression grandparents. We saw them scrimp, save, and cower at the thought of risking security for satisfaction — or even for greater security. We saw them live until they died — usually a short time after retirement — as if just living was enough. We decided we would not follow that path.

So, that brought us to a place where the Scarcity Paradigm died as its adherents died and the Psychedelic Paradigm offered only the chaos of unbridled experimentation.

The Debt Paradigm

The solution we devised has carried us deep into a labyrinthine economic paradigm that relies on false assumptions and produces the opposite of what it promises.

The first premise of the Debt Paradigm is that we can have everything we need and anything we want whenever we want it, if only — if only we are willing to *borrow* the money to get it.

The Debt Paradigm does not consider the possibility that we could have what we need and want without debt. In fact, the paradigm has created the myth that debt-to-others is good. We have allowed ourselves to be deluded into thinking that "need" and "want" are the same thing. The Debt Paradigm has convinced hundreds of millions of people that they need debt just as much as they need the "stuff" that they buy with debt dollars.

We have even become convinced that the best way to deal with debt is to get more of it. Not only can you "buy" your way to wealth, you can "borrow" your way to security.

Consider the oft-run television commercial where the hero, Stanley Johnson, is showcasing his family's up-scale home, new SUV, country club, swimming pool and riding lawnmower and he asks, "How do I do it?" He answers his own question by saying, "I am in debt up to my eyeballs. I can barely pay the finance charges." Then he pleads for someone to help him. The sponsor comes to his aid and promises that he can solve his problem. The solution is simple, Stanley. *Acquire some new debt* to "consolidate" your existing bills.

The implication in this commercial is that Stanley may lose all the good things in his life if he cannot meet his monthly obligations. That is scary for a generation that has become accustomed to having *creature comforts and status symbols without really owning them.*

The second insidious belief (implied in the first) that the Debt Paradigm instills and reinforces is that you can "buy" success, security and happiness. History and your own experience speak to the fallacy of this idea. If you define success as "having stuff" then success is for sale. Most of you would not accept that definition in a moment of clarity. You are, however, barraged daily with messages that promote this belief — advertising, store displays, at sporting events, and so on — all designed to distort your own sense of what is important to you. The goal of those who promote the Debt Paradigm is to have you act in their best interests not your own.

This introduces the third basic element of the Debt Paradigm — Corporatism. Corporatism is the belief that the larger an organization, the better able it is to determine what is best for you instead of you deciding for yourself. Your every day experience dealing with the Behemoths and current events like the Enron scandal, the WorldCom debacle, the thievery of Qwest execs, and the behavior of the unprincipled US Congress — all 535 of them — government employees and other elected officials is enough to demonstrate the foolishness of this premise.

The human side of this situation confuses the issue when you deal with an individual in one of these organizations. You want to trust the person even if you have the clarity not to trust the organization. The person you deal with, however, acts on the mandates of the organization s/he serves. The person may seem to act in your best interest and may believe that is precisely what is going on, when in fact s/he is limited in what is possible by the organization.

We will revisit all of the ideas introduced above as we progress through this book.

Now, let's talk about "economies."

Read on…

Chapter 4 – What Would Your Ideal Personal Economy Look Like?

"Industrial progress, mechanical improvement, all of the great wonders of the modern era have meant relatively little to the wealthy. The rich in Ancient Greece would have benefited hardly at all from modern plumbing: running servants replaced running water. Television and radio? The Patricians of Rome could enjoy the leading musicians and actors in their home, could have the leading actors as domestic retainers. Ready-to-wear clothing, supermarkets - all these and many other modern developments would have added little to their life. The great achievements of Western Capitalism have redounded primarily to the benefit of the ordinary person. These achievements have made available to the masses conveniences and amenities that were previously the exclusive prerogative of the rich and powerful." ~ Milton Friedman

Phase I – Let's Get Clear

Your personal economy is the microcosm of the larger economy within which you operate, so first let's review the definitions from earlier in the book. You will recall that we used two definitions for the macro-economy. The Encarta definition focuses your attention on production and consumption and the broader community:

Economy: The production and consumption of goods and services of a community regarded as a whole.

The Oxford Dictionary definition adds the concept of wealth and resources:

Economy: The wealth and resources of a community, especially in terms of the production and consumption of goods and services.

When these two definitions combined for purposes of this book, they become:

Economy: The application of the wealth and resources of a community, regarded as a whole, to the production and consumption of goods and services.

Applying this as a model for a definition of a personal economy, I devised the definition, which I use in this book — expanded here for clarity:

A Personal (or Family) Economy: The production of money (wealth and resources) by a family or an individual that is used (consumption) to acquire goods and services and to secure their future.

The definition of a family or an individual economy adds the element of future security to the definition. This is important. Macro economies have self-preservation built in. It is assumed that their diversity makes them self- sustaining. Being self-sustaining implies that economies at the macro level are not dependent on a single source for their "wealth and resources" or their "production and consumption," but that a fair amount of diversity is diffused throughout those economies.

American economic history gives us many examples of narrowly defined economies that failed because of their lack of diversity. Consider the coal towns of Appalachia that sprang up like spring flowers and wilted just as spontaneously when the coal ran out. Visit a ghost town in the west and you will discover that beaver pelts, gold or silver or some other one-dimensional economy was the beginning and end of the town. Consider the many small cities that the expressway system bypassed and, lacking the diversity brought by access, saw prosperity pass them by in the bargain.

Personal economies function analogously. A family or individual whose economy makes debt-to-others essential for its "wealth and resources" subjects itself to the wishes and whims of *The Three Money Monsters and the Behemoths*. A personal economy structured this way will eventually reach the same end as the ghost town's economy from America's past.

A personal economy needs to establish itself as a self-sustaining entity. It has to motivate behaviors that generate the momentum needed to keep itself going. This allows the family or individual to thrive in a diverse set of circumstances and to survive during the worst of times.

"But," you wonder, "where is this leading? How does it apply to me? What do I need to do to make sure I am not building a ghost town with my personal economy?"

Phase II – A Riddle

Economics deals with "production and consumption," "wealth and resources," and community. A personal economy deals with money. In economics, the individual and the family are consumers. In a personal economy, they are the producers. This creates a disconnect that needs to be clarified. How can a personal economy, lacking scale and diversity, adopt the same mantle as a larger economy? What is the commonality that even allows us to discuss a personal economy?

The answer does not present itself spontaneously. In fact, it is quite esoteric and the only way to find the answer is to traverse a labyrinth and discover the nuggets of wisdom and the clarity that are hiding there as well as discarding or ignoring the fools gold along the way. In addition, to make it more challenging, you must first solve a riddle to gain entry to the labyrinth itself.

The riddle is this: How is money like water?

Take a few moments and think about it. Make a list of your answers before moving on to the solution to this riddle.

_____

_____

_____

_____

The most common answer — almost 90% of the time — to the question "How is money like water?" is that money, like water, slips right through your fingers.

Other answers that come up frequently are:

☞ "You can't live without water and you can't live without money.
☞ "Money and water both flow.
☞ "Water comes and goes with the tides, the seasons, with weather changes and money comes and goes with changes in the economy, government, and just plain luck."
☞ "Water is everywhere and money is everywhere."

If you have come up with an answer that is not represented here, give yourself a pat on the back. These are the top five answers that hundreds of participants have given in dozens of seminars over the past few years.

Now you know the answers that others — and perhaps you — have given to this riddle. Those responses, however, do not earn you a pass into the labyrinth.

The answer that allows you to move from the riddle to the labyrinth is this: *most of the water on earth is in large and small reservoirs... oceans, lakes, rivers, underground moraines, ponds, puddles, teacups—even in your body. In a similar way, the money in the world is in large and small reservoirs...banks, credit unions, safety depositories, wallets, pockets, and tin cans buried in the back yard.*

Where do you think most of the water in the world is? If you guessed the oceans, you are correct. Over 70% of the earth is under water and over 95% of the water on earth is in the oceans.

Just as most of the water in the world is in the oceans, most of the money in the world is in — you guessed it — banks. When you get a paycheck where does it go? When you start your children on a savings program, don't you put their money in a bank savings account? When a corporation collects a payment, they put it in the bank. Insurance companies and investment firms that deal with trillions of dollars put those dollars into banks. Even local, state, and federal governments put their tax revenues in banks.

Phase III – Enter the Labyrinth

The various definitions of economies we've studied deal with wealth, resources, production, consumption and community, but don't say a word about banks; not a word about money. The reality, however, is that without money there are no banks and there is no economy. Economies run on money. Money is the fuel that empowers companies to produce and individuals to consume goods and services. Money is both the measure and the foundation of wealth. Nothing else is money — not stocks, not bonds, not mutual funds or 401(k)'s, not real estate, not even collectible wines — only money is money.

And we need the banks to control the money. This is not theory. It is a fact of life that each of us experiences every day.

Each step you take as you traverse a labyrinth is critical:

☞ Money is essential to economies. Communities almost always, and seemingly spontaneously, create a medium to measure and manage the production and consumption of goods and services. That medium, regardless of its form — gold, coins, currency, seashells — is generically called money. Barter systems precede the use of money, but work only in primitive economies and only on a very limited basis.

Barter systems fail because, as communities become larger and more complex, the relationships between the producers and the consumers within that system become more complex.

☞ Banks are essential to economies. There needs to be a mechanism and a structure to handle the medium used for measuring results and managing exchange in an economy; banks fill this role. Banks form when simpler systems fail.

☞ Banks, by their very nature, control most of the money in economies — even personal economies. As systems of commerce, production and consumption become more complex so also do the needs of the communities they serve. Both producers and consumers create banks to handle the money and the money system that they create.

☞ BUT — and this is a critical intersection in the labyrinth — *whose money is it that the banks control?*

If you recognize that it is your money, you are correct. Banks control the money that is essential to economies, but it is not the banks' money. It is depositor money — *your money.* (This doesn't deny that banks have money of their own. They're a part of the economy, too; they need money the same as you do…more on this later.)

Phase IV – Wander the Labyrinth

Stop and think about that for a moment. Banks control most of the money in an economy and it is not their money, but yours. If that does not cause you to question what the banks are doing with your money, then you missed the turn at the last intersection and may well be on a path into the clutches of a Money Monster, or the digestive track of a Behemoth.

Consider the question of what banks do with your money carefully. Banks control most of the money in an economy but it isn't their money, it's your money, your neighbor's or the money from your business. You voluntarily give your money to a bank. Why? Because you feel comfortable that the bank will take care of your money for you. You trust the bank to return your money to you when you want it. You are convinced that the bank will not lose your money.

What does the bank give you in return for your money? Sometimes they give you a bill to pay...checking account charges or transaction fees for example. Sometimes they pay you some interest — a few percentage points — in a savings account or certificate of deposit. *Regardless of whether you pay the bank or the bank pays you, what is really happening is that the bank is borrowing your money.*

When the bank has your money in an account, they do not just let it sit there. The entire business of a bank is to keep money moving and working. That is how the bank makes its own money. They lend it to someone at a higher interest rate than the rate they are paying you (their lender).

Some people think that banks "invest" depositor money. Investing entails, by its very nature, a risk of loss. Banks have kept the confidence of depositors for the many decades since the crash of 1929 by not "investing" depositors' money. Remember, the bank has to deliver your money to you on demand...whenever you ask for it. To invest your money would be to put it at risk, and that would be a breach of trust and possibly a breach of civil and criminal law too.

This brings us to another crossroad in the labyrinth.

☞ If banks prudently borrow money by offering depositors reasonable incentives to place their money in the bank and

☞ Consistently lend the money to their borrowing customers at a higher rate than they are paying you, the depositor,

☞ Then, it follows that banks do not lose money on the loans they make. And, this intuitive leap turns out to be true most of the time. The bank may lose some money on the occasional loan, but this is a relative rarity.

Consider the case of the repossessed car.[31] The businessperson bought a large SUV and the bank loaned $42,000.00 on the vehicle for 60 months at 7%.

☞ After 18 months, the bank repossesses the car.

☞ The balance due at the time of repossession is $30,900.00.

☞ The depreciated value of the vehicle, assuming a $48,000.00 purchase price and a $52,000.00 sticker is about $28,000.00.

☞ So, what does the bank, facing a $2,900.00 loss do? They sell the car at auction for $26,000.00.

☞ Have they lost money yet? Not really.

• They had already collected about $3,900.00 in interest at 7%, but had paid sinificantly less than that to the depositors whose money had funded the loan in the first place.

• In addition, they send a bill to the defaulting businessperson for the $4,900.00 difference between the auction price and amount owed…with interest added.

• If the businessperson does not pay this amount, the bank writes it off as bad debt along with accrued interest and all the collection costs. Then the bank sells

---

31 Statistics and information for this example were derived from BankRate.com and Edmunds.com.

the bad debt to a collection firm. The net of all this generates a tax deduction, further reducing the bank's potential loss.

The net result may produce a loss but banks are sophisticated. The business model they follow includes a factor for defaulted loans and their portfolio of loans seldom if ever loses — and, if it does, the losses are small and short lived. If they are not, the bank will be out of business.

In other words, banks employ the "Prudent Man Rule," which demands that banks use depositor money in ways that assure the return of that money on demand. The "Prudent Man Rule" is based on common law stemming from the 1830 Massachusetts court decision - Harvard College v. Armory. The "Prudent Man Rule" directed the trustees "to observe how men of prudence, discretion and intelligence manage their own affairs, *not in regard to speculation,* but in regard to the permanent disposition of their funds, considering the probable *income,* as well as the probable *safety* of the capital to be invested."[32]

---

32   http://en.wikipedia.org/wiki/Prudent_man_rule "Since the 'Prudent Man Rule' was last revised in 1959, numerous investment products have been introduced or have come into the mainstream. For example, in 1959, there were 155 mutual funds with nearly $16 billion in assets. By year-end 2000, mutual funds had grown to 10,725, with $6.9 trillion in assets (as reported by CDA/Wiesenberger). In addition, investors have become more sophisticated and are more attuned to investments since the last revision of the Rule. As these two concepts converged, the "Prudent Man Rule" became less relevant... ADDITIONAL COMMENTARY ...This discounting of the relevance of the prudent man rule is more the result of market forces than it is of the needs of individuals for "safety of capital." The 10,000+ mutual funds of 2000 have grown to over 15,000 mutual funds in 2006. Does any advisor claim to be expert on all of these funds? Does any one of the rating agencies promise that the funds they rate highly will perform better than those they don't? The Prudent Man Rule is even more important today than it was in 1830 if for no other reason than that the market has become so complex and no individual advisor or advisory firm can claim to be fully informed about the investments they recommend. Remember some former darlings of Wall Street; Enron, WorldCom, Global Crossing, Qwest?"

Imagine if your bank had invested depositors money in ENRON when it was the golden child of Wall Street. It may have made them look good for a while but in the end, it would have cost *you* a great deal of money.

> "But in the end, risk is risk, leverage is leverage, and miscalculation of risk is still miscalculation of risk." ~ Michael Lewitt of Harch Capital

Here's what is important:

- ☞ Money is like water in many ways. Most importantly, for this book, both money and water:
  - Slip through one's fingers
  - Are everywhere
  - Are a renewable resource
  - Are something we can't live without
  - Are constantly flowing
  - Are held in large and small reservoirs
- ☞ Banks control most of the money in the general economy around the world
- ☞ It's our money that the banks control
- ☞ Banks do not lose money on their loan portfolios
- ☞ Banks don't invest your money.

Hmmm.

Read on...

YouBeTheBank.com

Part 2
You Be The Bank

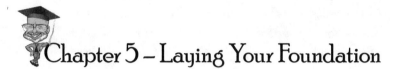

Chapter 5 – Laying Your Foundation

The Question at Hand

Now you know where banks[33] fit into the general economy. Perhaps you have thought briefly about where all this discussion is leading. You may have questioned yourself about your personal economy. You may be on the verge of formulating some critically necessary questions:

☞ Why don't we create a personal economy that emulates the general economy?

☞ Why don't we control the money in our personal economy the way banks control money in the general economy?

In simpler terms, why don't we handle our money the way banks handle depositor's money?

What does conventional wisdom tells us? This isn't a hypothetical question. In fact, it is a question that millions have asked and answered since the first escapees from the persecution of Europe's religious and feudal societies came to America.

---

33   You will find the term "bank" used frequently throughout the remaining chapters of this book. When the word is enclosed in quotes, it refers to a financial vehicle where you can safely put your money and still have control of it and ready access to it. This concept develops fully in the following chapters.

It is only in the past three decades since the adoption of The Debt Paradigm that Americans and others around the world have succumbed to the wiles of the Behemoths of Corporatism and bartered their liberty for the indentured servitude imposed by debt. In exchange Americans now *"have stuff" they don't own, and own investments they can't control.*

We've forsaken the independence that comes with being able to measure and manage our personal economy.

The most glaring macro-level examples of this situation are evident in government reliance on "lobbyists" and other money interests in Washington D.C. and in state capitals and other world capitals to formulate policy and legislation. The Congress is elected with dollars from the Behemoths and their minions — George Soros, the petroleum industry, the Hollywood "elite," 527's, and every other individual or PAC that has an ax to grind or a business to promote. The Presidency, governorships, state legislatures, county and city governments are the same. Big money elects people and Behemoths have big money. The Behemoths also have a vested interest in seeing their woman or man in an office where the goals of the Behemoth can be promoted.

At the micro-level, where you live, the Behemoths rely on marketing and advertising to convince you just as they rely on lobbyists and "experts" to convince gullible congresspersons.

If a Behemoth is willing to spend millions of dollars to send a 30-second message to you and the rest of America during the Super Bowl, then you know that they expect many times that in return. When an investment company tells you to buy their financial planning service by promoting it in ads every Sunday during some sporting event, or daily during a newscast, it is not because they want *you* to become wealthy. It is because they want to satisfy their investors and because the Behemoth's executives want to protect their jobs and their very large paychecks.

Executives earn huge salaries based on the performance of the company for the shareholders — not on whether or not the consumer gains anything. Obviously, there needs to be some real or perceived value or the consumer would not buy the products and services the Behemoths sell. It is important to recognize, however, that value is there *only* to produce growth and income for shareholders and that the focus is on perception, not reality. "Perceived benefits" are the issue. Reality is not an issue.

This is important: I am not saying there is anything necessarily unethical or illegal about what goes on in business or the general economy. We are not considering ethics, law, or even morality. The Behemoths are only doing what our society demands of them — producing the goods and services that society wants, or at least perceives that it wants, at prices that are affordable.

Conventional Wisdom and The Debt Paradigm

The issue is that the lessons the Bureaucracies and Behemoths are teaching you are *conventional wisdom* about *your role* in the overall economy.

- ☞ Remember Stanley Johnson — in debt up to his eyeballs — being advised to refinance his home to pay off his other debt?
  - • That is the lesson; that it is OK — perhaps even wise — to use debt to manage debt.

☞ The stock brokerage houses — online and otherwise — encourage you to do your transactions through them for a small fixed fee or online just before you rush out the door to the office or to coach a soccer game. Do they care if your transaction is successful or an utter failure? No. They make money either way.

- The lesson conventional wisdom wants you to learn is that it's easy to make money in the stock market if you pay low fees.

☞ The federal government has created a plethora of "retirement" plans. The IRS allows a tax deduction on most of them but recovers it later, after you retire — or earlier if you have financial challenges that you cannot handle with your income and other assets. The IRS recovers all of the taxes you didn't pay in the years you contributed to a retirement plan.[34] You pay the IRS either way.

- These federal programs teach you the conventional wisdom that a tax deduction today is more valuable than future income that is unencumbered by taxes.

☞ Do you think the "no interest and no payments until 2011" deal from the local furniture or appliance store is giving you any true value? Are interest free car loans a better deal than the $3,500.00 rebate? The Behemoths are not fools. They make money no matter which choice you make or what happens to you.

- "Don't you understand," they admonish, "that interest free or a big rebate is always your best deal? Hurry! Buy it today! Trust me."

---

34 Almost every client the author has served in his 30+ year career in financial services has invaded their "retirement" plan before they "retired" (some more than once), paid the taxes and penalties, and started over again.

☞ Is there any serious consideration given in conventional wisdom to creating a personal economy that is not subject to and controlled by the Bureaucracies and the Behemoths? Where does what *you* earn enter into their equation? Stanley Johnson says it best when he asks and answers his own question, "How do I do it? I'm in debt up to my eyeballs."

- Conventional wisdom is that your earnings are just a source of payment for "having stuff," repaying the debt-to-others you incur to get it and paying fees and commissions to the sellers of investments.

You can probably discover another dozen or so tenets of conventional wisdom in your everyday life that are designed to lead you deeper into the labyrinth of the Debt Paradigm and *further away from a personal economy that you can measure and manage*. In other words, the conventional wisdom of the Debt Paradigm encourages you to relinquish sovereignty over your personal economy and become the *indentured servant* of those who generously offer you *debt as your foundation*.

Here's an abbreviated outline of what the Debt Paradigm wants you to believe is important:

1. Get money…Earn/Borrow
2. Get what you need and want…Spend/Repay
3. Repeat this cycle *endlessly*
4. Bank a little so you can…
5. Spend It Later

…and maybe, *just in case*, you should buy some term life insurance.

Abbreviated further the Debt Paradigm looks like this:

Earn/Borrow/Spend/Repay.

Ask yourself "Is this sound 'financial planning?'"

No.

"Is it 'financial planning' at all?"

No.

"Without addressing the Federal Government's role and behavior, is there a single institution, Bureaucracy, Behemoth, or bank that itself follows this model?"

No.

"What is the difference between the principles articulated in The Debt Paradigm and what happens in the general economy? In particular, what do banks do that this model fails to do?"

Banks *borrow to lend*. The Debt Paradigm teaches you to *borrow to spend*.

A Zero Sum Game?

Controlling the money in the economy is not a zero sum game for business, government or for banks. It is, however, for consumers who have been lured into the labyrinth of the Debt Paradigm.

There are books that promote dying broke as the optimum zero sum outcome of a life. There are seminars, promoted by some financial advisors, which tell you to invest your way to security using annuities or mutual funds. They also suggest that you plan to go broke at an arbitrary age of 82 or 79. These ideas pay no regard to how long you actually live or what happens after you die.

There are courses in economics at major universities that support these bizarre ideas of how to handle the money that flows through your life. Financial advisor training often promotes these ideas (remember who designs and develops this training). There are books and seminars abounding that tell you that you can borrow your way to wealth and do it without any significant risk.

They are all wrong.[35] Your money goal in life is not to die broke and let posterity fend for itself. If that were the case, where would you be today? Where would America be?

Do you think that the Debt Paradigm — *Earn/Borrow/Spend/ Repay* — is the model followed by:

- ☞ Bill Gates?
- ☞ Oprah Winfrey?
- ☞ Donald Trump?
- ☞ Warren Buffet?
- ☞ The Walton family?
- ☞ The Rockefeller, Vanderbilt, or Carnegie families?[36]

Of course not. Each of these well-known successful people and families recognized that building a personal economy demands a foundation and framework that withstands the vagaries of time and the unpredictability of markets — all markets — and, that the path they follow continues beyond their personal destination.

---

35 There is a grain of truth in every "101" program or idea that is in the marketplace. The fallacy in most of them is that they present their approach as the single solution to money issues. In the old west, the snake oil salesman used the same tactic to sell a liniment that would heal everything that ailed you. In the world of today these "101" type solutions are no more valid than the latest diet fad or weight loss pill.

36 I do not claim to have intimate knowledge of the finances of those mentioned here. I draw the conclusion that they do not follow The Debt Paradigm from the results they produce.

For example, Warren Buffett recently gave much of his Berkshire Hathaway stock to the Bill and Linda Gates Foundation. The estimated final value of the gift is over $35 *billion*. Bill and Linda already fund the Bill and Linda Gates Foundation at over $30 *billion*.37 Posterity.

A Digression

Please, do not imagine that I am about to take you on a fantasy tour of your "possible" life of luxury — a life based on some "if only" proposition:

- ☞ if only you would live up to your potential;
- ☞ if only you would take advantage of the opportunities that present themselves daily;
- ☞ if only you would buy some miracle-promising set of books or tapes or adopt the practice of the successful seminar mouthpiece.

You might be able to accomplish as much as Gates, Buffett, Winfrey, Trump, or Walton. You may not. You — like these icons of financial success — may be the rare individual that achieves world changing results and acquires world-class wealth.

You may also become a Mother Teresa, Gandhi or Martin Luther King who produces equally extraordinary world changing results in another aspect of living but whose personal financial successes are trivial or non-existent in comparison.

You are a uniquely talented *and* uniquely limited individual. You may not be able to attend to more self-focused money goals until your special needs child is able to care for her/himself. Your abusive spouse

---

37 Fortune Magazine, by Carol J. Loomis, FORTUNE editor-at-large, June 25, 2006.

may have killed your spirit and you have yet to regain it. Your destructive parents may have distorted your self-image and you are in the process of clarifying it. You may just be the kind of person who needs a lot of time to decide on what is important in his/her life and, like Grandma Moses, achieve greatness and wealth very late in life.[38]

Regardless of your circumstances, however, you can do better than you are doing today. More than likely you are one of the many: you work hard to care for those you love, provide for them as best you can as the breadwinner or the caretaker or both, and wonder why some other person, who seems no more capable than you, succeeds where you feel you fall short—even though you probably don't fall short at all considering your individual circumstances.

There are thousands of motivational seminars, books, tapes and CD's that can help you achieve more than you feel you achieve now. There are many personal coaches who will address your need for motivation, time management, goal setting, activity planning, budgeting, debt reduction and almost any other aspect of your personal or business life. There are hundreds of viable part time businesses that you can operate — some in partnership with your spouse and children. Your pastor, rabbi, lama, imam, or psychologist may provide guidance and help you.

Each of these programs and people would expect that you, if you expect to make any real progress, *first become aware* of your deep-seated (paradigmatic) beliefs that hold you back. If you gain nothing else from this book, that awareness is a major benefit and will serve you well for the rest of your life

---

38   http://en.wikipedia.org/wiki/Grandma_Moses Grandma Moses started painting in her 70's and continued successfully into her 90's.

The Money for Life Model

You should have the same expectation of yourself when it comes to how you deal with your money. Expect yourself to have the courage and will to become aware of your self-defeating beliefs and to rebuild your personal economy on a new base.

By becoming aware of the failures and fallacies of the Debt Paradigm that you (and most other Americans) have incorporated into your thinking and decision-making, you open yourself to other alternatives. Through awareness, you begin to deconstruct your version of the Debt Paradigm, which currently rules your use of money, so you can rebuild your personal economy on a stronger foundation and with a sturdier framework.

The Debt Paradigm tells you to earn, borrow, spend, repay, repeat that cycle endlessly, and, as an afterthought, bank a little so you can spend it later.

The Money for Life Model makes a subtle and essential change to the failed Debt Paradigm when it introduces the idea that lets *YouBeThe-Bank*.

You can operate your personal economy with the same practices that banks use and then create the same results banks create; practices that are the foundation of every fortune — no matter how small or large:

- ☞ Get money — earn it, inherit it, win the lottery, sell "stuff," invent (just don't rob the bank)

- ☞ Bank it — put it someplace that will allow you to act as your own "bank"

- ☞ Borrow from *your* "bank"

☞ Spend what you borrow to buy the things you need and want

☞ Repay your "bank" both the principal you borrowed and the interest on the money you borrowed

While the Debt Paradigm teaches you to passively accept servitude to the Money Monsters and the Behemoths, The *Money for Life* Model trains and guides you to master your money for yourself and for posterity!

The How To

So far this discussion intentionally leaves practical questions unasked and unanswered in order to smooth your "paradigm shift" from the Debt Paradigm to The *Money for Life* Model.

☞ Remember what the "conventional wisdom" of the Debt Paradigm unabashedly and incorrectly tells you about how to handle your money:
- you can buy your way to wealth
- you can borrow your way to wealth
- you can have everything you need and anything you want as long as you have enough "credit" (translated, that's debt for you)

☞ Remember Stanley "up to my eyeballs in debt" Johnson? Become aware of the fallacies that permeate Debt Paradigm thinking. Recognize that your first responsibility is to yourself and your family not to the Behemoths or the Bureaucracies.

The Bureaucracies and Behemoths want your money, and not just some of it, they want all of it. Look at what happens when you get a paycheck or you calculate the income from your business.

First, there are taxes: FICA, income tax withholding, Medicare, state tax, city tax. The sad thing is that the taxation doesn't stop at the pay stub. In fact, if you were to itemize all the taxes you pay you would want to include property taxes, sales tax, taxes on your telephone service, utilities, gasoline and on and on. Therefore, your pay just decreased by as much as 50%: about 40% to withholdings of various sizes and shapes and 10% you'll pay out in dribs and drabs as you spend the balance.

Then you have to pay your first mortgage, your second mortgage, or equity line of credit, credit cards, auto loan payments, charge cards from department stores and other big box retailers.[39] For many Americans that's as much as 35% of their paychecks, leaving little or nothing for food, medical care, clothing, utilities, phone, education, transportation, vacations, entertainment, and the like. But, let's say that you are among those who still have control of at least a small amount of their income. If you are typical, that means you have about 11% left over for those essentials.

If you replace these percentages with numbers, an American family with two working spouses might earn $60,000.00 a year or $5,000.00 per month. About $2,500.00 each month goes to taxes in one form or another. $1,950.00 goes to interest and debt reduction (mostly interest). That leaves about $135.00 a week – about $19.00 a day - for food and other essentials. If that isn't enough, guess where the family goes to cover the shortfall: equity lines of credit, credit cards, and so on... Debt.

You may have noticed that there is no provision for personal or retirement savings in this budget. In 2005, the savings rate for

---

39 One of the most insidious "taxes" that you pay is the interest you pay on the taxes you finance when you buy something on credit. The taxes are included in the total you pay and you pay interest on the taxes – a double whammy.

Americans was a negative (-.5%); in 2006 it was still negative (-.1%). The only other time in our history that Americans have had a negative savings rate was during the great depression (1932-33). The reason then was an economic downturn of unprecedented proportions. The reason today is the Debt Paradigm. In other words, for the first time, Americans have *internalized the causes of their negative savings pattern.*

Even people who participate in defined contribution retirement schemes like 401(k)'s, SEP's or Paradigms are often in a negative savings pattern. These individuals put money into their tax qualified retirement plans at a slower rate than they spend borrowed money from credit cards and home equity. Thus, they incur interest charges, which mount steadily until they are in debt up to their eyeballs — just like Stanley.

What's a person to do?

Conventional wisdom spouts platitudes that sound meaningful, but are really intended to capture your money. Conventional wisdom tells you to save 10% of your income. Why? So you can spend it later.

Conventional wisdom tells you to max out your 401(k). Why? So you can pay taxes later – probably at a higher rate than the tax saving rate of the deduction you took.

Conventional wisdom tells you to invest in real estate, stocks, mutual funds, and so on. Why? Because every time you buy or sell anything, someone else earns some of your money. Whether you make money or build wealth is irrelevant to the Behemoths and Bureaucracies because they are making money from your transactions.

Most significantly, conventional wisdom does not tell you that if you do what it recommends, the Behemoths and Bureaucracies gain control of you and your money; that you no longer have free access to your money.

If you buy an investment, the only way to get your money out is to sell the investment. If you lose money when you sell, you get back less than you spent. If you gain money when you sell, you have taxes to pay. Either way, the investment no longer exists. It becomes cash and the cash, in many cases, pays debt while the investment's earning potential no longer exists. In addition, someone else handles your transaction when you buy, and again when you sell, and earns commissions or fees, even if you lose money.

"But wait" you say, "I can borrow against my investment or other assets."

That's true, sometimes. However, even if you borrow at a rate that is less than the investment return at the time the loan is initiated, the borrowed money significantly reduces the value of that return. If the return on the investment goes down or the interest rate on the borrowed money goes up, (or both) you lose. Moreover, there is no guarantee that you can borrow at all, since the Behemoths get to decide if you are "credit worthy." Therefore, to get to your own money, you're frequently stuck with only one choice, selling your investment.

I hope you are scratching your head by now and wondering where in the world can you "bank" your money so that you can use it without having to sell an investment, or borrow against an asset, and pay interest to someone else so that you can use what is, after all, *your own money.*

Before launching into this discussion and how becoming your own "bank" works and benefits you and your personal economy, take a few minutes and ask yourself the following questions about building a personal economy. Take stock of both the answers that come to mind and how you feel when you see yourself as the master of your money:

☞ Would you agree: You have two roles to play when it comes to money: one is the role of income producer in the vocation, career, or business you have chosen; the other is being the *master of your money* — being your own banker?

☞ Would you agree: Nobody taught you how to be your own banker until now?

☞ Would you agree: It is just as important that you learn to be your own banker as it is to learn the skills you need to succeed as an income producer?

☞ Would you agree: If you fail to *master your money* and you do not become your own banker, it may lead to:
- failure as an income producer
- failure as a provider
- failure as a parent
- failure as a spouse

☞ Would you agree that *it is essential* that you learn to master your money and become your own banker?

Being the Bank

If you answered "yes" to the questions posed in the last section, congratulations! You have abandoned the Debt Paradigm. You are ready to embrace *The Money for Life Model* and to become the *master of your money and your own banker.*

☞ To be the *master of your money,* you need to know where you can put *your money* so you can use it: without selling or otherwise liquidating assets

☞ paying interest and fees to others

☞ while enabling you to manage your money the way banks manage money

☞ and build your own personal economy by building your own "bank."

Get Money

Let's start with a discussion of how being your own banker works. You'll remember the first element of the short formula used earlier — Get Money.

When you think of the money that flows into your personal economy from your work, your business, or even your income producing investments, it is important that you *not* think in terms of gross income or earnings. Think instead of the net after-tax dollars you can deposit in a bank, yours or someone else's. Remember that you must feed the Dragon — the taxing bureaucracy.[40] For this discussion, you need to focus only on building a foundation and framework to support your current and future money related decisions.

It is also important that when you calculate the net income you can put into a bank, you *include* the voluntary contributions you are making to retirement plans, health insurance, and other deductions from your net earnings through your employer or your business.

Even though you may not currently have access to this money, it is still important to recognize that it is your money and that you get to decide how you are going to employ that money from this point on. You may well find that these dollars are doing the job you want them to do and that you don't need to make any changes. But, you may also discover that you need to make adjustments in order to escape from the grip of the Debt Paradigm.

---

40 In Volume II of this series you will learn more about how to manage this monster.

In addition, consider the money and other assets that you control — savings certificates, mutual funds, real estate, automobiles, recreational vehicles, equipment, retirement accounts and so on — that you could convert into money to put in your "bank."[41]

Now you've "got money."[42] It may be a little money or a lot of money. The amount of money you can put in your "bank" is not a major issue in terms of the process — although I recognize that it is important to you. You will likely discover that you have already allocated most of your money to other uses based on lessons taught by the Debt Paradigm. Questioning those decisions is an important part of this exercise but is not a reason for feeling bad. This is just the first step and you will discover that you can and will overcome the failures of the Debt Paradigm as you progress.

The next step in building a personal economy is to —

Bank It

Put it into your "bank." Let's see how that works.

When you put your money into a commercial bank, the professionals at the bank manage the use of your money in order to guarantee you the return promised by the bank. If they are following the Prudent Man Rule discussed earlier, they will lend your money to borrowers that can reliably repay those loans.

---

41 Remember, only money is money. Stocks are stocks, mutual funds are mutual funds, real estate is…you get the picture. You can only spend money. You must first convert, one way or another, every other asset to money if you wish to make it available for your needs and wants.

42 Appendix B is a worksheet that will help you identify your sources of money and evaluate how you are currently using your money.

Your "bank" should work the same way. When you open your "bank" you shouldn't have to find qualified borrowers and execute loans. Your "bank" should also have professionals that perform these functions and make loans, by combining your money with that of other small "banks," to businesses and individuals with outstanding credit ratings, for mortgages and to other businesses for other legitimate business purposes. This assures the repayment of any loans made using the money from your "bank" pooled with the money from other "banks."

"Wait a minute!" you think, "I don't need my own "bank" to do that. That's what commercial banks do anyway when they accept my deposits at a specific rate and lend the money to others at a higher rate."

You are correct, and here's where being your own banker becomes interesting. The commercial bank works for the benefit of its owners (its shareholders if it is a publicly traded company). *Your "bank" should work exclusively for you.* When a commercial bank lends money and earns a profit, its net worth increases and it pays a dividend to its owners or shareholders, while you receive only a small interest payment. When *your* "bank" lends money and earns a profit, your net worth should increase and any dividends that are paid, should be paid to you.

Borrow from Your "Bank" to Buy
What You Need and Want

As incredible as that is, it is not where your "bank" serves you best. When you go to a commercial bank to obtain a loan, you must "qualify." Even if you pledge assets equal to or greater than the amount of money you want to borrow, you have to qualify. Even if you are borrowing to buy an asset that is of greater value than the loan you are requesting, you have to qualify. Even if you are an owner of stock in the bank or an officer of the bank, you still have to qualify. In addition, qualifying means you have to tie your assets to the loan to protect not you, but the bank.

When, on the other hand, you borrow from your personal "bank" you should be able to borrow up to the amount you have in your account without a need to "qualify" in any way. You simply have your banker write the check — no questions asked, no qualification required, no additional assets needed for collateral. And, here is the truly amazing part: even though you borrow all of the money from your account, whether you applied that money to one of your life goals or used it for something entirely frivolous, as you repay yourself, your net worth should continue to grow, as if you had not borrowed a penny.

"How is that possible?" You ask. "How can I have use of my money and still have it working for me? How can my money do double duty like that?"

It is possible only if your "bank" treats your loan the same as a loan to Microsoft or Toyota. If your money were on loan to those corporations, your account value would remain the same, interest would accrue, and dividends would continue to add to the value of your account. A loan to you is, in this regard, the same as a loan to another entity. A loan does not diminish the value of the account from which it is drawn because the money will be paid back, *with interest*.

There would be, however, differences between you and those other borrowers.

- ☞ When your "bank" lends money to others, your banking system would require periodic repayment from those debtors.
  - When *you* borrow from your "bank," you should be able to create the repayment schedule that best suits your needs.

☞ If the other borrowers default on their loans, your account would not suffer because your banking system has built in protection against losses.

• If you do not repay the loans you grant yourself, your "bank" would eventually go broke and pass out of existence.

☞ Your banking system would set the interest charged on loans to others.

• The interest you charge yourself would be up to you. (You will discover shortly, that it is better to overcharge yourself than to cheat your "bank" by paying yourself less than your banking system charges others or less than the banking system needs to keep itself running profitably.)

Repay Your "Bank"

When you borrow from a commercial bank, use a store charge card or a credit card to purchase an item, the bank pays the merchant, you take the item home and repay the bank, including interest, over a specified period of time or in periodic payments of specified minimums. At the end of the repayment period, the bank has recovered all of its money and all of the interest you paid and you have a depreciated, and in many cases worthless, item. In other words, you gave your money away in exchange for nothing of real value.

When you borrow from your "bank," you repay the entire cost of the purchase and all of the interest to yourself.

Take the example of a purchase that has limited residual value such as furniture. If you were to finance a $5,000.00 sofa using your credit card and repaid the loan and 12% interest in twelve months, you would have spent a total of $5,330.88 and you would have a comfortable and attractive couch that is worth little or nothing in a resale market.

On the other hand, if you had borrowed the $5,000.00 from your own "bank" and repaid yourself the exact same amount you would have paid a commercial bank, you would have the $5,330.88 in your own "bank," and you would still have the sofa. In other words, you would have recovered the cost of the sofa and the interest you paid and put the entire amount back into your own "bank" where you could borrow it and pay for your next purchase.

What's the difference? In terms of out of pocket payments, there is no difference between repaying a commercial bank and repaying your personal "bank." The difference is that when you own the "bank," you — not a commercial bank – have realized the profit in the transaction and recovered all of the money that you used to purchase the item — and you still own the item. Over time and the many purchases you make in your lifetime, this adds up to substantial amounts of money sitting in your "bank." More about this later.

The question that arises for many at this point is, "How can I start a 'bank?' I don't have a lot of money."

If you start a commercial bank you need a lot of money. In many states, you need about $5 million to start a bank and the approval process takes up to five years. You are not starting that kind of bank, however, and you do not need a lot of money to begin. What's important is that you recognize that you can begin to lay a foundation for a sustainable future where you control the money that flows through your life.

Every financially successful person has a "bank": money that is entirely under their control with no strings attached to Behemoths, Bureaucracies, or Commercial Banks. The Debt Paradigm has stolen the belief in this basic idea from America and American families. In its place, the Debt Paradigm has insinuated the belief that debt is the answer to achieving the American Dream — that you can have everything you need and anything you want as long as you have the credit needed to buy it. The Debt Paradigm is a house built on sand. It will not survive.

Whether you can afford to start your "bank" with $1,200.00 a year, $12,000.00 a year or $120,000.00 a year, you have to start in order to free yourself from the *indentured servitude* to the Behemoths and Bureaucracies into which the Debt Paradigm has lured you.

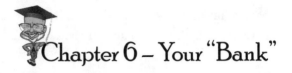

Chapter 6 – Your "Bank"

It won't surprise you that only a limited number of savings, investment and insurance products let YouBeTheBank. It shouldn't surprise you then that most financial and investment advisers — and certainly the banking entities that rely on you paying interest — don't talk about these products, and especially about this process.

Almost any financial product that allows you to access your money can serve as a "bank." Let's take the example of the $5,000.00 sofa discussed earlier. If you were to use a savings account as your "bank," you could withdraw the $5,000.00 from savings and create a repayment schedule that would create the same $5,255.81 in your savings account that would have accrued in that account had you not withdrawn the money.[43] So, by financing the sofa yourself you would recover not only the interest you would have paid to a lender, but also the principal.[44] If you pay yourself a higher interest rate — say the same 12% your credit card charges — you'd have $5,330.88 in your account at the end of the year.

---

43   Rates and results acquired from BankRate.com 8/21/2007 using a 5% savings account rate available from several banks.

44   Ibid.

You could use the same strategy with a bank CD, but you would also have to make sure you repaid yourself any penalty and taxes you may have incurred because of an early withdrawal.

If you decided to use money you had invested in stocks, bonds or a mutual fund, you would have to track the fund's performance and repay yourself accordingly. You would also have to account for the tax implications and any fees charged by the fund and, perhaps most importantly, if the fund lost ground during the repayment period you would have to make up for the loss out of your cash flow to assure yourself a reasonable return and restore the investment to its full value.

Using a 401(k) account as a "bank" can sometimes make sense. You can normally borrow some amount — often about 50% — of your 401(k) account value. Some plans only allow loans for specific purchases, such as the purchase of a home. Usually there are limited restrictions on the uses for the money and you can repay your account on a schedule that suites you and at a fixed interest rate. The challenge with this approach is the same as the one presented above where we discussed using investments. A 401(k) has the added disadvantage of creating a possible negative tax result if you terminate your employment before you can repay the loan in full.

If you are a Baby Boomer or younger it may surprise you to discover that cash value life insurance products provide the best opportunities for you to be your own banker. Here is a bit of background to give you some perspective.[45]

---

45 Appendix C references a well thought out comparison between banks and insurance companies with a special focus on their performance during the Great Depression.

What Your Parents Knew

A recent survey asked people younger than 60 years old a series of questions about their lives compared to their parents' lives. The survey showed that, in almost every aspect that could be measured, those taking the survey were better off than their parents: houses were bigger, education was more advanced, income and net worth were higher, possessions such as cars, furniture, boats, etc. were more plentiful.

The one aspect of life that the study showed did not measure up was *peace of mind*. The parents of the boomers were all seen to have less economic stress and more composure when if came to money. I believe the reason for that is debt-to-others. While the parents of those surveyed had less "stuff" — even less income — they also had more savings and *much less debt*. They were more secure.

The survey did not address where the savings of this older generation were and did not take into account the wide range of social and economic differences between the generations. It clearly highlighted this important difference, however: the older generation was more at peace with money and was better able to deal with unplanned and planned life events.

Keeping these facts in mind, let's look at where the older generation kept their money. First, the older generation was more inclined to savings and safety than to investment and risk. Much of the money that the older generation accumulated was in home equity, savings accounts, guaranteed income pension plans and in guaranteed cash value life insurance; and most of the money in life insurance policies was in dividend paying whole life insurance from mutual life insurance companies.

Based on almost four decades of experience guiding people through the maze of contradictory and confusing claims about money, I find one thing to be true: those clients who relied on whole life insurance as a foundation for their personal economies and their "banks" lived more securely and with less worry than those who did not. In addition, our parents were able to build more wealth and to pass on more of their wealth to their heirs. This is just as true today as it was 30, 40 or 50 years ago. This reality contradicts the conventional wisdom that permeates financial plans that rely on term insurance and investments.

There are several reasons why dividend-paying whole life insurance from a mutual company worked so well as a "bank" for prior generations and works just as well today.

- ☞ Policyholders own mutual life insurance companies.[46] The executives and employees who work in mutual companies work for the individuals and families who own policies sold by that company.
- ☞ Mutual companies, therefore, operate exclusively for the benefit of their policy owners. They are not beholden to outside investors, individual or institutional shareholders. The bottom line for mutual companies is how well they serve their owners — the policyholders.
- ☞ Since mutual companies pass their surplus earnings on to their policyholders, the *IRS treats mutual companies as non-profits*. Their earnings are exempt from taxation.
- ☞ If a mutual company didn't distribute all of its profits to the policyholders and owners each year, they would jeopardize their mutual status, subject policyholders to significant tax risk, and violate the basic tenets of their charter.

---

46   Some of the most respected and financially stable insurance companies are "mutuals": Mass Mutual, NY Life, Northwestern Mutual, The Guardian Life Insurance Company, and other lesser known but equally safe and reliable companies.

☞ Mutual companies historically maintain low operating expenses. Unlike their non-mutual counterparts, mutuals don't have to devote significant monies to investor relations, to taxes and to other expenses related to their competitors' status as taxpaying corporations.

It is not just mutuality, however, that motivated and supported the decisions of older generations to make whole life insurance an integral part of their money structures and that continues to recommend it today. The whole life product itself[47] offers unique advantages not available in any other insurance, savings or investment vehicle.

Scrooge and Marner Bank

Consider this conversation with Mr. Silas Marner, the not-so-friendly banker at Scrooge & Marner Bank.

You speak:

"Good day Mr. Marner. Thanks for taking time to speak with me today about the purchase of an asset of *real property*. Mr. Marner, the property I want to purchase is valued at $1,000,000.00. Here are the terms I would like to have for this purchase…

☞ First, I want to purchase this property with *no down payment*.

---

47 For a comprehensive discussion of the various types of life insurance and a thorough discussion of how each works you can consult the 3rd edition of *Tools and Techniques of LIFE INSURANCE PLANNING* by Stephan Leimberg and Robert Doyle; published by The National Underwriter Company, pp 1 – 269. Please, do not rely on the abbreviated discussions and definitions found on internet sites as they can't, in the space and time they devote to it, convey enough of the information you would need to understand this complex and evolving product. It is even less likely that you could find enough information on internet sites to make an informed decision about which type of insurance might suit your situation best without the expert guidance of a mature and well-trained professional.

☞ I also want to purchase the property *without any credit check* and based solely on my willingness to commit to level monthly payments.

☞ I want your bank to guarantee that those payments will never increase.

☞ I want a *guarantee from the bank* that the property will never decrease in value.

☞ I want any growth in equity value to be tax free.

☞ If I decide later that I no longer wish to own this property, I want the bank to *guarantee that the equity I have built up will be paid to me in cash or as a lifetime income that I cannot outlive* and that the property will revert to the bank at no cost to me.

☞ If I decide that I don't wish to make payments for some period of time *I want the bank to automatically make those payments for me as a loan* against my equity at a guaranteed rate of interest.

☞ If I want to borrow against my equity for any reason, I want the bank to make the loan without *question or qualification*.

☞ If I do borrow, I want the bank to only charge me a *guaranteed rate that we agree upon before signing* the purchase application – even if the loan is requested years into the future – and I want the bank to accept any payments I make, even if they are less than enough to repay the loan.

☞ If I die prematurely, before the property is fully paid for, I want the bank to pay my heirs *the entire $1,000,000.00, less any loans I have taken, regardless of how many payments I have made* – even if I die in the very first month after purchasing the property.

☞ I want to be able to make extra payments and I want the bank to keep track of them for me.

☞ Finally, Mr. Marner, I want to pay the bank a few extra dollars each month so that if I get sick or hurt and can't work the bank will make my payments for me.

So, what do you think Mr. Marner; do we have a deal?"

Silas Marner speaks:

"NO! No to everything. Such foolishness is wasting my time. My bank doesn't work that way."

Hmmm! A conventional banker finds these terms ludicrous. However, if you were to apply those questions to a whole life insurance contract from a mutual company, the answers would all be 'Yes!.'"

It's true, you can purchase a $1,000,000.00 asset that

☞ requires only that you qualify medically,
☞ guarantees a tax free increase in equity each year,
☞ has a guaranteed level monthly payment,
☞ allows you to take a loan against its equity at will, at a guaranteed rate and that you can repay on your own terms,
☞ assures your heirs full value of the asset less any outstanding loans,
☞ promises to pay your premium if you are sick or hurt or just can't make a payment for whatever reason.

Wouldn't a "bank" like that be valuable to you?

"But wait!" as Billy May, the TV product spokesman for everything from Oxyclean to picture hangers, says "There's more!"

Dividends

Mutual companies are innovating a completely new generation of more flexible and more powerful whole life products to meet the needs of the 21st century. In addition, mutual company whole life policies pay dividends.

Dividends add an entirely new dimension to the discussion of why a whole life policy makes a great "bank" and is fundamental to a money structure that you can expect to endure.

First of all, dividends from stocks that you own are taxable. Dividends paid to mutual company policyholders are considered a return of unused premium that has already been taxed and are, therefore, paid tax free and grow tax free as long as they remain with the policy.

Unlike reinvested stock dividends, a whole life contract guarantees that you'll never lose the dividends you leave in the policy. If you were an MCI, Qwest or Enron shareholder and reinvested your dividends, you know what I mean — you lost them in the end along with the rest of your investment.

A mutual company traditionally pays dividends from a whole life policy each year on the anniversary of the policy.[48] You can take your dividends in several ways based on your instructions to the insurer.[49]

---

48   Many policies do not pay dividends in the first few years after issue. Older, well-established mutual life insurance companies have long histories of paying dividends even during difficult financial times such as the Great Depression.

49   Some new policy designs add other options for the use of dividends but these are not yet available from all companies and on all policies so we are not including them in this discussion. Your financial guide will be able to identify these options for you.

☞ The simplest is payment in cash. You can instruct the insurance company to send you a dividend check each year.

☞ You can have the dividends reduce your out of pocket premium expense, by instructing the insurance company to use the dividend to pay some or the entire regular policy premium.

☞ A third option is to have the dividend placed in an interest bearing account that the insurer maintains on your behalf. If you choose this option, the earnings on the account are taxable.[50]

☞ The most beneficial option, however, is to use the dividend to purchase additional single premium life insurance, called paid-up additions:

- The paid-up additional insurance death benefit requires no qualification of any kind. It requires no proof of insurability and no need to justify the additional death benefit.

- The cash value of the dividend used to purchase the paid-up insurance becomes a guaranteed cash value and enhances the cash value of the basic policy.

- The paid up additional insurance cash value grows unencumbered at the same rate as the base policy and pays dividends itself as long as the policy is in force.

---

50 Dividends that you take as cash, to reduce premium or that you leave to accumulate interest are tax-free until the total of the dividends you receive is equal to the total of the premiums you have paid. After that, you'll pay taxes on the dividends you receive. Proper planning by your guide might allow you to receive future dividends tax-free as well. Consult your guide and tax advisor before making these decisions to assure the best outcome for yourself.

- The dividend paying practice that works the best as your "bank" pays dividends on the base policy and also on the paid up additional insurance, even when the policyholder has borrowed money from the policy. If, for example, your policy had accumulated a cash value of $50,000.00 and you borrowed $40,000.00 to buy a new car, the policy dividend would be the same as if you had not borrowed a penny.[51]

- There are, finally, no commissions paid on additional insurance purchased with dividends so all of your dividend dollars, minus only a small set-up charge, go to work for you immediately.

Other Kinds Of Cash Value Life Insurance

Traditional universal life insurance and interest sensitive whole life insurance and more recently, equity indexed universal life insurance are also vehicles that can be used as "banks." Policies in these categories do not, however, have the same borrowing options as participating whole life insurance, and lack the guarantees that permit whole life insurance to produce its superior results for those who use it as their "bank." It is possible to use some of these products in the "banking" process but the results over a long period are not yet proven. I do not recommend them at this time.

There is an entirely new wave of life insurance products coming to the market that are based on the 2001 Commissioners Standard Ordinary

---

51 Not all insurance companies pay dividends this way. Some pay only on un-borrowed values. This makes a difference in the way your policy accumulates value but even the policies that pay dividends only on un-borrowed values perform well as "banks" in relation to the alternatives.

Table (CSO Table) of life expectancy.[52] Some of these products are next-generation whole life policies and others are embracing some of the capabilities of traditional whole life. It will take a few years to sort out which might be valuable to the insurance "banking" concept. Stay tuned.

Variable universal life insurance utilizes underlying investments that put the policyholder at substantial risk and lacks the guarantees of even the universal life products. It is not suitable for this application.

Dividend paying whole life insurance from a mutual company is the only product that is proven over time to let YouBeTheBank and control the money that flows through your life. In the following chapters you will see a variety of examples of how the "banking" practice works in a well constructed personal economy. All of these examples employ dividend paying whole life.

---

52   The CSO Table is revised every 20 years or so by the National Association of Insurance Commissioners (NAIC) from each of the 50 states.

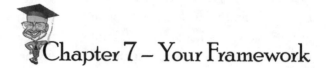

Chapter 7 – Your Framework

The Four Pillars

☞ **The First Pillar** — freedom from debt-to-others

☞ **The Second Pillar** — money when you need it to replace lost income or because expected and unexpected life events such as job loss, medical expense, home or nursing home costs put you in a financial bind

☞ **The Third Pillar** — an income you don't have to work for and you won't outlive

☞ **The Fourth Pillar** — a legacy of wealth and wisdom for those you care about.

The sections of this chapter illustrate how the Four Pillars contribute to the gift that you give yourself when you adopt The *Money for Life* Model — peace of mind about money. The examples used in each section are not extreme but they may not even remotely reflect your situation. Don't let it concern you.

The first step in the process of changing your mind about money is to take apart your unique financial structure and then put it back together to better serve your needs. One person might focus initially on debt elimination; another's focal point might be reorganizing assets; someone else may choose to pay attention to spending patterns to free up cash flow. You may decide to address several of these issues at once.

Consider also that each person starts from a different place. Some could only find a few dollars each month for their first "bank." Some of those same families today have built solid foundations and erected each of the Four Pillars to suit their needs. At the other end of the spectrum, there are families and individuals who put $10,000.00, $50,000.00 or more per year into their "banks."

Most people who adopt The *Money for Life* Model are just like you, however, and find ways to rebuild their money structures to serve their current and future needs based on their unique situation.

There is no standard way to break an old paradigm down in order to adopt a new one. The principles that underlay the illustrations used in the following pages can be helpful when you pay attention to how those principles fit your unique situation.

The first step is to develop awareness. Awareness is essential to the mind and practice altering decisions that allow you to master your money and escape the indentured servitude of the Debt Paradigm. Don't worry about whether or not you fit the examples. There is a lesson that may apply to you in each of them.

One final thought before we start. The Four Pillars are presented in sequence throughout this book. I do not intend to suggest that one money concern is more significant than another. You may find that money concerns surrounding health issues outweigh the debt issues in your life. Someone else might place their attention on creating a legacy, while for yet another person or family, income may be first on their agenda.

The beauty of The *Money for Life* Model is that it adapts itself to the needs and concerns of each person, and doesn't rely on the rigid formulas of computer software, or the conventional wisdom designed by and for some financial Behemoth.

The Foundation and the Four Pillars let you measure and manage all of the money that flows through your life. You can use your money for your purposes — whatever they may be — depending on your needs at any given point in time. The construct does not tie you to a sequential approach.

Finally, be aware that the practices this section illustrates depict ideal situations — no family crises, no financial setbacks, no business failures. Life doesn't work that way. The *Money for Life* Model allows you to respond to less than ideal situations, however. If something goes awry in your life, your personal economy will respond effectively.

Read on...

The Framework – The Four Pillars
The First Pillar – Freedom from Debt-to-Others

> "When you live on cash, you understand the limits of the world around which you navigate each day. Credit leads into a desert with invisible boundaries." ~ Anton Chekhov

Let's begin with a real life example of how to start your "bank" and what the long-term results might be.

Most likely, you buy automobiles. If you are a typical American you trade your "old" automobile for a new one every third year, and your payments increase each time you trade.

Since you are reading this book, either you do not follow this model or you may want to change that behavior. So, let's create a slightly different set of assumptions.

- ☞ First, assume that you have a car that is three years old and that you just made your last payment – you hold the title not the bank.
- ☞ Further, assume that your payments were about $550.00 each month.
- ☞ You can also assume that you have cared for your car and that it still has low maintenance life in it so you can drive it for another four years. [53]

---

53 A recent article in Car and Driver quoted on the auto pages of MSN states that today's automobiles can operate for over 200,000 miles with little or no maintenance beyond the periodic scheduled maintenance prescribed in the owner's manual. I personally can testify to this with one small 1993 sedan with 190,000 miles on it that still gets the same gas mileage it did when new and a 1992 SUV that has almost 160,000 miles on it. Both vehicles are pretty much trouble free.

☞ Looking forward, assume that for the next four years you are going to put the $550.00 that you would normally pay each month to buy a car into your "bank" instead.

☞ Finally, we assume that you finance $24,000.00 each time you buy a car.

Now, based on those assumptions, let's look at the result of buying a car every four years for the next 40 years — ten cars. We'll consider three buying strategies:

1. Borrowing $24,000 every four years from a commercial lender each time you buy a car and repaying that loan in four years. If you finance your ten cars using conventional financing costs, you'll spend about $272,000.

2. Using the CD method as your "bank," you would save $550 each month in advance of each purchase and pay cash for each car. This allows you to accumulate about $112,600 in savings over the same period and still buy the cars.

3. Funding your life insurance "bank" in the first four years, just as you saved using the cash method, then borrowing from your own "bank" and repaying yourself during each subsequent four-year cycle, you end up with over $507,000 in your "bank." That's a gain of over a $750,000 in net worth over the financing approach— and you would not have spent a single penny more buying your cars than you would have spent financing your cars at a commercial bank.[54]

---

54 As with all projections of future costs and financial growth, nothing is guaranteed. Some but not all of the elements that contribute to the growth of the "bank" are projections based on past performance, are contingent upon the overall performance of those managing your money and could produce greater or lesser results. Results are not, therefore, guaranteed. So also, interest rates used in calculating loan payments and savings returns came from BankRate.com. Future interest rates may be substantially higher or lower than those used in the calculations. Since all of the assumptions used in this illustration and throughout this book are drawn from information obtained from reliable sources, you can expect that, even though they are not guaranteed, their credibility is high.

In graphic form it looks like this:

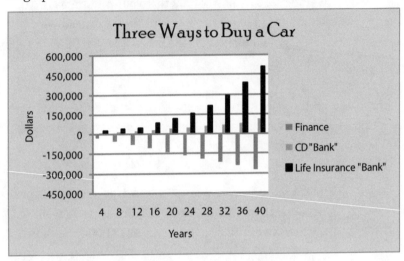

Let that sink in for a moment.

Now, consider how this same process would add to the money you get to keep for yourself when you buy appliances, furniture, or other large ticket items. This proven strategy can pay for vacations, your kid's education, or any other product or service that you would normally use credit to purchase. Let yourself become aware of the economic power you exercise when you are the "bank."

Imagine your peace of mind knowing that you control the money that flows through your life and that you can use the extra money in your car "bank" for other purposes as needs arise.

Remember, becoming the "bank" is not a short-term project; it is a way of life. You can begin immediately and, in a few short years, grow the money that you control to the point that you will be able to eliminate debt-to-others in every aspect of your life. Eventually you may even be able to convert your mortgage from a debt-to-others into a debt to your "bank" and recover the tens of thousands of dollars that you would otherwise pay to mortgage lenders by re-paying yourself.

John and Mary

Here's an example.[55] A young couple (John, age 27 and Mary, age 26) purchased their first home for $200,000.00. The house appraised at $245,000.00. Their credit ratings were good so they were able to finance 100% of the purchase price.

The couple had saved $20,000.00 for the down payment (which they didn't need) and planned to use this money to decorate, furnish and landscape the house. Had they followed this path, they would have transformed $20,000.00 cash into bushes, paint, and light fixtures and that money would have been entirely unavailable for any other purpose.

Instead of following this self-diminishing plan, they put the money in a "bank"...actually two "banks." They deposited $10,000.00 into a "bank" for John and $10,000.00 into Mary's "bank." They then went shopping for their decorating, landscaping and furnishings and carefully completed the entire project for just under $12,000.00, which they charged at a variety of stores. In each case, they qualified for a one year same as cash payment schedule. Six months later when the money in their "banks" was available, they borrowed $12,000.00 from themselves and paid off the interest-free debt-to-others incurred in decorating, furnishing, and landscaping their new home.

They chose to pay themselves back at the rate of $300.00 per month including interest, so they repaid the loan in less than four years, and they recovered all of the money they had spent.

---

55   John and Mary are a fictional couple and will appear in the following pages as we point out the uses for your "banks."

However, that's not the end of the story. In addition to repaying the loan they had taken from their "banks," they continued to add money to their "banks" at the rate of $700.00 per month. Just four and one half years later their "banks" had a loan free balance of over $50,000.00. The loan on the house had only reduced to $185,000.00 during this same period based on the $1,200.00 per month payment, so John and Mary decided to use the $50,000.00 from their "bank" to reduce the mortgage loan. They also decided to refinance the remaining $135,000.00 and reduce their mortgage payment to just over $800.00 per month. They continued to put $700.00 into their "bank" each month. They found their incomes increasing so they began paying the $50,000.00 loan from their "bank" back at the rate of $800.00 per month also. In just about 6 years, John and Mary recovered the entire $50,000.00 they had borrowed from themselves and they had a balance in their "banks" of over $120,000.00 – enough to pay off the entire mortgage and hold a clear title to their home in fewer than 11 years.

That, however, left John and Mary with a debt-to-themselves of $120,000.00. They decided to pay themselves back at the rate of $2,000.00 each month. Just over 5 years later, they had recovered all of the money they borrowed from their "banks," including interest that they would otherwise have paid to a mortgage company. They also continued to add $700.00 to their "banks" each month during this time.

The bottom line: John and Mary paid off a $200,000.00 mortgage and put over $200,000.00 into their "banks" in just 16 years. Between the money in the "bank" and the equity in their home,[56] John and Mary created an estate value of over $600,000.00. If John and Mary

---

56 This assumes a conservative 4% rate of appreciation on their home yielding a value over $400,000.00 in 16 years. 4% is the rate assumed by HUD when it does its calculations.

continued to contribute to their banks at the same rate and continued to live in the same home until they were at retirement age (another 24 years) and did nothing else to improve their money situation they'd have about $1,300,000.00 in their "banks" and over $1,000,000.00 in home equity assuming a 4% appreciation rate.

I recognize that the transactions described above with words and numbers may be hard to visualize, so here's a spreadsheet that illustrates them. The spreadsheet reflects the amounts paid or contributed during the given year and the balances owed or accumulated at the end of each year.[57]

---

57   Calculations were developed in late February 2007 and are based on information from BankRate.com and from MassMutual Life Insurance Company - reference footnote 26 above.

Mortgage Example

End of Year	Mortgage Payments	Mortgage Balance	"Bank" Deposits	"Bank" Loan Balance	"Bank" Repayments	"Bank" Cash Balance
1	14,400	197,544	24,200	10,200	1,800	9,505
2	14,400	194,937	8,400	6,600	3,600	20,567
3	14,400	192,168	8,400	3,600	3,600	29,082
4	14,400	189,229	8,400	0	3,600	41,250
5	14,400	186,106	8,400	0	0	52,874
6	60,706	133,332	8,400	41,506	9,600	20,337
7	9,600	131,582	8,400	31,906	9,600	39,100
8	9,600	129,713	8,400	21,306	9,600	59,070
9	9,600	127,729	8,400	11,706	9,600	78,750
10	9,600	125,823	8,400	1,106	9,600	100,655
11	9,600	123,387	8,400	0	9,600	124,399
12	123,387	0	8,400	99,385	24,000	24,266
13	0	0	8,400	75,385	24,000	72,660
14	0	0	8,400	51,385	24,000	104,684
15	0	0	8,400	27,385	24,000	143,920
16	0	0	8,400	3,385	24,000	183,933
17	0	0	8,400	0	0	204,050

"Wait a minute!" you say. "No one in their right mind would just let $200,000.00 sit in their 'bank' when they could use it to finance the life and lifestyle they were working so hard to build."

That's a great observation and raises a great question, "What next?" Before we address this question, however, remember that all of the money in the "banks" that make up The Four Pillars is also an integral part of your Foundation and you can apply that money to any goal you choose.

Example: John and Mary have two children

In year 17, when they have paid off the home loan from their "banks," John Jr. is 15 and Miriam is 13. Both children are good students and plan to attend college. They could make their plans based on acquiring traditional student loans. It would be better if they borrowed their education expenses from this or another family "bank," and repaid the family "bank" instead of some Behemoth. If they do that, they would replenish and enhance the family "bank" and some Behemoth would lose out on all that interest. Later, that same "bank" could finance the children's first homes.

Debt-to-others

By now you recognize that unless you have a substantial amount of money exclusively under your control, you are probably unable to deal with the harsh realities that even predictable events send your way, without putting more debt-to-others onto your personal balance sheet. That may be good for some credit grantor, but it is not good for you as an individual or for your family.

This is not news.

If you were to speak with hundreds of people as I do each year, you would soon discover that perhaps as few as 1 in 1,000 are prepared for the expected, much less the unexpected. You would also discover that almost every one of them is currently facing or has recently faced a financial challenge and many of them are starting over from scratch. When you probe further you would discover that the way many of them dealt with past challenge was with new debt-to-others.

That's the Debt Paradigm; you can have everything you need and anything you want as long as you have enough credit. The problem is that eventually people run out of credit. When that happens, they either tighten their belts to start paying down their debt, or they head for the attorney's office to begin bankruptcy proceedings.

It's easy to imagine the fate of those who opt for bankruptcy. Morris filed bankruptcy when his business failed after he had invested all of his personal assets in it. A few years later Morris had recovered just enough to get a sub-prime mortgage and buy a newer car from a dealership that operated a buy-here pay-here finance company.[58] He valiantly continued his quest for the things he could buy with debt-to-others and, as you might imagine, soon found himself in front of the bankruptcy judge again.

Most people who file for bankruptcy reform their ways just long enough to re-establish their credit. They then drive right back into the heart of the Debt Paradigm. A few choose to reform their thinking and behavior but, without the guidance of a seasoned professional, are eventually drawn back into the unrelenting lava-flow of the Debt Paradigm. A rare few choose to work with a professional advisor and adopt practices that allow them to remain forever free from the fear of bankruptcy.

Those who decide to solve their money problems as the Debt Paradigm suggests, by getting more debt-to-others — like our old friend from the TV commercial, Stanley Johnson — delude themselves into believing that they've solved the problem. What has really happened is that the pain and pressure imposed by debt-to-others has been pushed

---

58   Some independent auto dealers sell cars to individuals with limited resources and finance the car themselves or through a subsidiary at a higher than normal interest rate to offset the possibility of losses incurred when a buyer defaults. Frequently the buyer must make payments personally at the dealership.

below the surface, allowing the underlying problem to grow worse and worse almost unnoticed, except for the long, sleepless nights and undiagnosed exhaustion and depression.

Debt-to-others is as addictive as the most vicious drug. Believing that you can deal in debt-to-others without becoming addicted is as naive as believing you can use crack cocaine without becoming an addict.

There is a valid exception to this scenario. You can use debt consolidation as a starting point to escape from the grasp of the Debt Paradigm. This rather sophisticated strategy appears simple but requires you to start your "bank" at the same time you are reducing and eliminating your debt. You'll want to discuss this strategy with a professional guide if you are currently trapped in the Debt Paradigm and you decide to move courageously beyond your comfort zone and the dictates of "conventional wisdom."

Future volumes from the *Money for Life* series will deal with the "how to" of these more advanced strategies. For now, just remember that every dollar that's in your "bank" is under your control, and if you apply those dollars wisely, you will have more money every December than you started with in the preceding January.

The Second Pillar – Money When You Need It

Aging America

Most Americans are not aware of a looming money crisis in their lives.

Ed and Edie were in their late 70's. Ed had retired from a small manufacturing company. Ed's company didn't have a retirement program, but Ed had managed to accumulate about $250,000.00 during his working years. Using only the earnings from their very conservative investments and savings, plus Ed's Social Security, the couple lived a comfortable but not extravagant life.

Then Ed began forgetting things, and was soon diagnosed with Alzheimer's disease. Within eighteen months, he was in a nursing home and Edie was saddled with the tasks of managing the money, the house and — everything.

That created a new set of problems. Edie had never driven a car, mowed the lawn, or even written a check. The couple's children lived too far away from Mom and Dad to help out on the day-to-day basis that would have been ideal. Their oldest was the closest, and he lived over three hours away and could only come to help on weekends. The other siblings, each with a family to care for and support, could only help with occasional visits and some small monetary contributions to help defray the growing expenses.

Edie's health deteriorated rapidly under the stress. She was in the nursing home with Ed within a year. The expenses depleted the resources in the family home, and all of Ed's and Edie's other assets. Shortly thereafter Medicaid took over. Ed lived another year and Edie followed him within months — with a broken heart and a broken spirit. The children were devastated by the loss and by the frustration of being unable to do more for their frail and aging parents.

Most aging Americans face significant future medical and long-term care expenses. Fidelity Funds publishes a report annually that projects the out of pocket medical expenses a retiring couple should expect during their remaining lives. In 2007 that amount was $215,000.00 — 7.5% higher than in 2006. Do the math. You will soon realize that ten years from now, at the same inflation rate, you could be looking at $450,000.00 of unfunded out-of-pocket medical expense. Add to that the possibility of long-term care expenses over an increasingly long life span, and you could easily arrive at a million dollars or more of unfunded future liability as a retiring couple.

The Unpredictable

Even if you are on the right track, like John and Mary in the previous chapter, there are unpredictable events that could dramatically change the picture. What if Mary developed Multiple Sclerosis (MS) and had to leave her lucrative position as the principal of a junior high school? What if she required significant at home care? What if John had worked as an accountant for Enron and found himself looking for a job during a significant downturn and with credentials that were questionable because of his prior association? What if both of these events occurred simultaneously? Even with their best-laid plans, they could be in serious financial hot water.

Let's presume, however, that John finds work with a reasonable income within a year, and that the costs of caring for Mary can be managed with the benefits from her education career. It becomes clear that by having "banked" over $200,000.00 and having paid off the mortgage so that their expenses were minimized, John, Mary and the children could deal with the unexpected, recover from it, and continue to pursue their lives with some lifestyle adjustments, but without significant money problems.[59] Here's the information we developed for John and Mary in the previous section.

---

59   Proponents of systems like those described in *Missed Fortune* by Douglas R. Andrew would suggest that paying off the mortgage is a foolish thing to do. I am not debating the efficacy of that practice but simply illustrating what might happen if the given circumstances prevailed.

			Mortgage Example			
End of Year	Mortgage Payments	Mortgage Balance	"Bank" Deposits	"Bank" Loan Balance	"Bank" Repayments	"Bank" Cash Balance
1	14,400	197,544	24,200	10,200	1,800	9,505
2	14,400	194,937	8,400	6,600	3,600	20,567
3	14,400	192,168	8,400	3,600	3,600	29,082
4	14,400	189,229	8,400	0	3,600	41,250
5	14,400	186,106	8,400	0	0	52,874
6	60,706	133,332	8,400	41,506	9,600	20,337
7	9,600	131,582	8,400	31,906	9,600	39,100
8	9,600	129,713	8,400	21,306	9,600	59,070
9	9,600	127,729	8,400	11,706	9,600	78,750
10	9,600	125,823	8,400	1,106	9,600	100,655
11	9,600	123,387	8,400	0	9,600	124,399
12	123,387	0	8,400	99,385	24,000	24,266
13	0	0	8,400	75,385	24,000	72,660
14	0	0	8,400	51,385	24,000	104,684
15	0	0	8,400	27,385	24,000	143,920
16	0	0	8,400	3,385	24,000	183,933
17	0	0	8,400	0	0	204,050

With these hypothetical situations in mind, refer back to the money concerns in the introduction that we all must face; consider your own situation today:

☞ Do you face challenges at work that could affect your income and force you to rely on your savings?

☞ Do you have aging parents who might need your assistance and support?

☞ Could your budget handle an unexpected major expense such as a new roof or replacing a car? How about two at the same time?

☞ Do you have enough savings to allow you to be out of work for a year or more?[60]

☞ What would happen if you were totally disabled and unable to work for the remainder of your life?

☞ Have you developed the money resources to deal with your own unfunded medical and long-term care expense — today and as you grow older?

☞ Are your children looking forward to college without athletic or academic scholarships so they — or you — will have to foot the whole bill?

In other words, have you prepared for the expected and the unexpected? Can you take care of your family's needs without incurring debt-to-others?

---

60 You might plan to replace six months income at age 25. As you grow older and have a family to care for you should have readily available money to pay your bills for 3 to 5 years. If you are over 50 and looking for work in your chosen profession, you might go for two or three years before you give up and take a job that is well below your education and skills qualifications, so your current lifestyle and your future retirement income may suffer drastically if you have only 6 months or a year's expenses set aside.

Disability and Long Term Care Insurance

"Look forward with confidence so you don't have to look back with regret." ~ Dr Agon Fly

One of the least pleasant and therefore most ignored aspects of managing money deals with what happens to you if you become totally disabled and/or require ongoing assistance with the activities of daily living.[61]

This is pure risk management. Just as auto or homeowners insurance protects you from an improbable loss of assets, disability and long term care insurance[62] protect you and your family from the unexpected loss of your greatest assets: your ability to earn an income and the money you are relying on for future income.

This is not an easy dilemma to resolve. The cost of disability insurance ranges between 2% and 4% of income, and is generally not tax deductible. Therefore, a person earning $60,000.00 a year might have to spend $2,400.00 a year for a disability policy that would pay about $36,000.00 per year in benefits. Long-term care insurance costs vary greatly but can be $10,000.00 or more per year for a couple in their 60s who choose benefits that will last their lifetime.

---

61   The Federal legislation that qualifies individuals for Medicaid long term care services and recognizes long term care insurance policy premiums as tax deductible specify six "activities of daily living" as qualifying factors.

62   Typically, disability and long term care insurance are bought separately and may or may not overlap; i.e., disability insurance is normally purchased by younger people and is replaced by long term care insurance at older ages. In some cases, long term care insurance benefits are incorporated into disability insurance contracts and several companies that sell both kinds of insurance have programs that allow you to transition from disability insurance to long term care insurance relatively seamlessly.

One solution that works extremely well, however, is to set up one of your "banks" to fund first the disability and later the long-term care insurance premiums. This strategy is quite complex and demands close attention to the details but it allows you to recover all of the premiums you pay over your lifetime.

Here's an outline of how this approach might work to fund a long-term care program for a 55-year-old man and his 51-year-old wife. The illustration shows cumulative cost:

A funding idea for Long Term Care Insurance

M55/F51, $6,000 per month benefit increasing at the compounded rate of 5% per year, 30 day waiting period, $5670 per year premium

Male Age	Option 1 Premium Paid Annually	Option 2 Single Premium Annuity	Option 3 "Bank" Account (Cumulative Values)		
			Cash In	Cash Value	Net Cost
56	5,670	93,381	12,980	5,583	7,397
57	11,340	0	14,620	2,426	12,194
58	17,010	0	22,291	9,727	12,564
59	22,680	0	29,962	17,337	12,625
60	28,350	0	37,633	25,271	12,362
75	113,440	0	115,364	158,766	-43,402
85	170,100	0	107,951	184,112	-76,161
100	255,150	93.381	115,967	215,339	-99,372
Lost opportunity cost calculated at 6% net:					
	1,278,631	1,285,353			859,022

Option 1 represents the cost if the couple never filed a claim and paid the $5,670.00 premium annually until the husband reached age 100. If this were the situation and both spouses were still alive, the premium would continue until their death. If the couple fell on hard times and couldn't afford the premium any longer, the policy would either lapse or provide a significantly lesser benefit.

Option 2 illustrates the cost if the couple funded the premium by purchasing a single premium annuity for $93,381.00 that would pay them a $5,670.00 annual income for as long as one or both spouses remained alive. This option assures that the money to pay the premiums is available but it doesn't assure that the couple will use the money to pay those premiums since they could use the income to pay for anything.

Option 3 shows using a "bank" to fund the premium payments and to ensure that the policy remains in force for as long as the couple lives. Option 3 also returns all of the money the couple paid into the plan if they chose to terminate the program after the 12th or 13th year or when they die…regardless of whether or not they ever needed to use the benefits of the long term care policy.[63]

To compare the costs in the first two options to Option 3 you can use the "Net Cost" column in Option 3 as the basis of comparison. To compare values you only need to recognize that the first two options deliver no value other than the protection provided by the long-term care insurance, while Option 3 delivers over $215,000.00 in cash at age 100 and continues to throw off enough income to keep the policies in force for as long as the couple chooses.

---

63   Ref footnote 33.

There is one more important element to this discussion. If one or the other spouse becomes eligible for benefits under the terms of the policy we used to illustrate this concept, the insurance company waives the premiums for both spouses. This would end the premium payments under Option 1, free up the $5,670.00 annuity payment under Option 2 so it could be used for any other purpose and, add significant value to the policy used to fund Option 3.

Afterthought

You may already have recognized that this Pillar is the most complex and challenging to deal with because it addresses a great variety of situations. You may also surmise that you may need several "banks" to deal with its various aspects.

Don't let that deter you. It is not an impediment to your success. In fact, each "bank" that you establish becomes a reliable source of money for you and your heirs that you can tap into as your present and future needs demand. In addition, it is often possible to fund a new bank with an existing one — but that's a strategy for those who have an experienced guide and who are true masters of their money.

The Third Pillar – Income You Do Not Have to Work For and You Will Not Outlive

Money for Life is not just about avoiding debt-to-others and being prepared for any life event, whether expected or unexpected. It is also about being prepared for your predictable short and long-term money needs, as well as your future income needs.

Social Security

Social Security currently pays a maximum of $2,116.00 per month to workers who earned the maximum taxable amount of $97,500.00 for 40 quarters during their working years. The typical retired worker, however, receives only about $1,050.00 per month and retired couples who both paid into Social Security earn about $1,700.00 per month.[64]

I believe that Social Security is a reliable source of income for future retirees. Many other advisors, individuals, and pundits do not have the same level of confidence and suggest that you should not consider Social Security benefits when looking forward to the time when you will need income that you don't have to work for, but won't outlive. There are a wide range of opinions on the possible outcomes to this issue, so you'll have to weigh all the options in your own mind to come to a decision. This is not a judgment call that anyone can make for you.

One strategy for dealing with Social Security that seems a reasonable compromise is to include Social Security in your plans as a back up to the other plans you adopt. Since Social Security is a government

---

64   Figures for 2007 - http://www.ssa.gov/pressoffice/factsheets/colafacts2007.htm.

program and is subjected to the whims and wishes of our not-always-brilliant, and sometimes-downright-dumb Congress, putting it in a subordinate position to the passive income[65] that you exclusively control makes a lot of sense.

Other Passive Income

Regardless of whether or not you include Social Security in your plans, your freedom today and in the future depends on whether or not you create a source of income for yourself and your family that you don't have to work for and you can't outlive.

Let's take another look at John and Mary from previous sections. You'll remember that John and Mary had used their "bank" to pay off their mortgage and accumulate over $200,000.00 in cash by the time they were in their early 40's. You may also recall that, if they did nothing else between that time and their normal retirement age, they would have over $1,300,000.00 in their "bank" and over $1,000,000.00 in equity in their home.[66] Here's what their situation looked like after 17 years.

---

65   Passive income normally refers to income you do not have to work for such as rental income from investment properties or dividends from stocks and bonds. In this context passive income refers to income that you do not have to work for and that you cannot outlive.

66   Ref footnote 33, pg 76.

End of Year	Mortgage Payments	Mortgage Balance	"Bank" Deposits	"Bank" Loan Balance	"Bank" Repayments	"Bank" Cash Balance
		Mortgage Example				
1	14,400	197,544	24,200	10,200	1,800	9,505
2	14,400	194,937	8,400	6,600	3,600	20,567
3	14,400	192,168	8,400	3,600	3,600	29,082
4	14,400	189,229	8,400	0	3,600	41,250
5	14,400	186,106	8,400	0	0	52,874
6	60,706	133,332	8,400	41,506	9,600	20,337
7	9,600	131,582	8,400	31,906	9,600	39,100
8	9,600	129,713	8,400	21,306	9,600	59,070
9	9,600	127,729	8,400	11,706	9,600	78,750
10	9,600	125,823	8,400	1,106	9,600	100,655
11	9,600	123,387	8,400	0	9,600	124,399
12	123,387	0	8,400	99,385	24,000	24,266
13	0	0	8,400	75,385	24,000	72,660
14	0	0	8,400	51,385	24,000	104,684
15	0	0	8,400	27,385	24,000	143,920
16	0	0	8,400	3,385	24,000	183,933
17	0	0	8,400	0	0	204,050

Since John and Mary are following *Money for Life*[67] practices, they would not simply allow their bank to grow passively for the next 20+ years. They would continue to borrow from their "bank" to buy the things the family needed, and to repay the "bank" to assure its survival and free up earned income for other investments.

For example, John and Mary could invest the $24,000.00 they used to repay their "bank" every year for the next 20 years in an equity-

---

67 This strategy employs insurance, savings and investment products structured to eliminate downside risk for the investor and to provide income for life regardless of what happens in the markets. This strategy assumes a 6% rate of return.

based product like a mutual fund or a variable annuity. Assuming the investments grew at a cumulative and conservative 7.2% net return, John and Mary would accrue over $1,100,000.00 dollars in separate accounts without adding to or depleting their existing "banks" in any way.

Combined with their "banks," but excluding the equity in their home, John and Mary would have about $2,400,000.00 with which to produce income they would not have to work for and they could not outlive.

In fact, if John and Mary were to apply the *Money for Life* strategy they could draw about $144,000.00 per year income — much of it tax free — from their "banks" and their side account without touching any of the principal. Moreover, if the principal continued to grow at the rate of 7.2% ($172,800.00 per year) John and Mary would gain inflation protection so the $144,000.00 would also grow each year. Toss in Social Security income of about $36,000.00[68] per year and our couple should be able to live quite comfortably for many years.

---

68   This assumes that both John and Mary have contributed less than the maximum but more than the average to Social Security or that Mary's retirement plan from teaching produces about the same as Social Security.

Reverse Mortgages[69]

First, a reverse mortgage is an acceptable and ethical way to use the equity in your home without creating a drain on your cash flow. In addition, a reverse mortgage does not put your home or your estate at risk. If you are not familiar with reverse mortgages, you'll find clear and understandable information at the National Reverse Mortgage Lenders Association web site.[70]

Reverse mortgages are powerful weapons in the money-arsenal of people over the age of 62. When John and Mary have both reached the age of 62 they will qualify for a reverse mortgage. A reverse mortgage is one of the best and least cumbersome wealth and income building strategies for those of us who have accumulated more years than we wish to acknowledge. In John and Mary's case, they could get a reverse mortgage on their home that could create up to a $500,000.00 equity fund that could grow annually or could generate another $25,000.00 to $50,000.00 after tax income per year.

---

69   A reverse mortgage can serve your goals for each of The Four Pillars. If you find yourself in debt buying cars or paying for essentials with credit cards, and you have a small mortgage and substantial equity in your home or your home has no mortgage at all, a reverse mortgage can eliminate your first mortgage and those debts by drawing equity from your home. The nice thing about this type of mortgage is that it doesn't burden you with a monthly payment and can even provide you with a monthly income.

  »   Many times the proceeds of a reverse mortgage pay for long-term care insurance, domestic services in the home of a frail elderly person or for medical care that is not covered in other ways.
  »   Reverse mortgages may also serve your desire to create a legacy. Many people have used this tool creatively to transfer assets from their estate to their heirs.

70   http://www.reversemortgage.org.

Combining all of these strategies, John and Mary could reasonably expect an income, which they do not have to work for and that they cannot outlive, of $200,000.00 per year or more.

And remember that John and Mary achieved this result with almost no investment risk, by following the *Money for Life* methodology.

The Fourth Pillar – A Legacy

"What you leave behind is not what is engraved in stone monuments, but what is woven into the lives of others." ~ Pericles

Creating a legacy of both your wisdom and your wealth is the most essential component of The *Money for Life* Model. The *Money for Life* Model Seminar, which articulates the basic principles found in this book, addresses the Fourth Pillar — Legacy — first; and, the first principle of Legacy is to teach the principles of The *Money for Life* Model to your children and your grandkids. Of what value is wisdom that you hoard and do not share? Of what value is your wealth if it dissipates when you die?

It is, of course, possible that you will die without having accumulated great wealth or significant assets to pay forward. The goal is not to create a legacy at your own expense. You need first to take care of yourself, your spouse, and your dependents. But, if you have gained the money-wisdom that allows your family — or whoever your beneficiary might be — to build their wealth and control their money, and you have passed that on, your gift of money-wisdom is of far greater value than any mere money you could leave to your heirs.

The Bike

Here's an example of how one man passed on the Legacy. Mr. and Mrs. Smith started a "bank" for their only son when he was born. They funded it in anticipation of the boy's future needs.

When Junior was 11 years old, he came to Dad very excited about a bike he had seen advertised. (I remember that feeling. For me it was a Schwinn with a chrome headlight prominently displayed in a store window.)

"Dad" he said, "there's this really cool bike at the ABC Bike Store, and Dad, if I had this bike, it'd be the coolest bike on the street and I really want it Dad."

"How much does this bike cost, Junior?" Dad asked.

"Wellllllll...ummmm...I think it's kinda 'spensive, Dad" Junior replied and he handed Dad the newspaper ad.

"Nine hundred dollars is a lot of money for a bike, Junior," said Dad with a bit of surprise in his voice.

Then, after a long pause, Dad said, "I think it's time for you to learn about money, Junior. When you were born, your Mom and I started a "bank" for you. We still own the "bank," and the money in it is there to help you learn about *Money for Life*. It's time for your first lesson."

Dad explained to Junior that he could borrow the money for the bike from his "bank," and that he would have to repay the money he borrowed. Then he taught Junior the basics of interest and payments.

When Junior objected that he didn't have any way to make the payments, Dad reminded him that he received an allowance to buy his lunches, to buy birthday gifts, go to the movies and so on. He could decide to use that money differently if he really wanted the bike more than those other things. Dad also offered to pay Junior extra money if he agreed to do some chores on a regular schedule. Junior would have enough income to pay back his "bank" at the rate of $33.00 per month — including interest — in just less than three years and still have some money left over for other things.

The bargain was struck, and Junior got the coolest bike on the street. When the other kids saw the bike they were amazed and wanted one just like it.

"How much did your Dad pay for it?" they wanted to know.

"Dad didn't buy it for me" Junior replied, "I borrowed the money from my own 'bank' and bought it myself for over nine hundred dollars."

Imagine how Junior felt. His bike made him feel proud. His "bank" enhanced his self-esteem. You know which of those is truly important. The bike will rust. Self-esteem turns into gold: not just financial gold but moral, ethical and relationship gold as well. Junior went on to finance his first car at 16 and repay himself. He then used the "bank" to fund a large part of his college costs and repay himself. He'll soon be buying a new car...and financing it himself...while the money in his "bank" is growing tax-free. In addition, Junior always recovered both the principal and interest in his "bank" that he — or his dad — would otherwise have paid to a commercial lender.

Think about how much tax-free money Junior will control in another 50 years and the kind of financial kick-start his children and grandchildren will have because he learned about *Money for Life* when he bought the bike at age 11.

> "What is important for kids to learn is that no matter how much money they have, earn, win, or inherit, they need to know how to spend it, how to save it, and how to give it to others in need." ~ Barbara Coloroso

That is *legacy*.

"But I'm 32 (or 46 or 59)," you say. "It's too late for me."

That's an excuse not a reason.

One family I recently advised, a husband and wife who are both 63 years young, recognized that they might have almost as many productive years in front of them as they have behind them. They are starting their "bank" to help finance their current lifestyle, to stave off future medical and long-term care expenses, and to create and preserve a tax-free legacy for their grandchildren.

I could tell you any number of stories about clients of all ages and in a wide variety of life situations who found that *Money for Life* is

- ☞ a superior way to control the money that flows through their lives and
- ☞ the best way to create a meaningful legacy.

John and Mary from prior chapters began their "banking" practice when they were in their mid twenties. R. Nelson Nash, one of the leading proponents of the practices we discuss in this book, was about 50 when he first realized the power of *Money for Life*, and was in his 70's and retired before he started in a significant way to teach others.

Paul was 35, just married and in a new business when he started. He was barely able to contribute to his "bank" during the first few years. Now, Paul is planning to increase his contributions to his first "bank," and to start a second "bank" for his soon-to-be-born son.

Wisdom Is Wonderful but What About the Money

Passing on your wisdom is the first principle of the Fourth Pillar. Paying your wealth forward tax-free is the second.

Many planners today either encourage or accept that maturing couples — sometimes with multiple marriages and blended families — discount the possibility, or even the desirability of leaving a money legacy. The consensus is often that "the kids can take care of themselves." While it is true that many find themselves unable to incorporate a significant money legacy into the plans drawn by some financial advisors, it is also true that if they incorporated the practices of *Money for Life*, those same couples and individuals might be able to both improve their current lifestyle, and create a tax-free legacy.

Here's one example. Bill and Sally were about to retire. Bill's retirement plan was quite good and Sally had some IRA money that they could rely on. After they purchased long-term care insurance, made provisions for future medical expenses, secured a reverse mortgage and conservatively managed the balance of their assets to achieve the income they desired, they still felt that their income and reserves were barely going to last them the rest of their lives. The children were relatively successful. They would not be expecting an inheritance, so Bill and Sally decided that they would not make provisions for a legacy of money.

When Bill and Sally thought further about it, however, they recognized that they would very much like to leave some sort of inheritance to the grandchildren they adored. A little tweaking and some fresh thinking led them to establish a dynasty trust71 to benefit the grandchildren as well as future generations. Bill and Sally invested very little to initially fund the "banks" in the trust. The trust, however, assures that their children, their grandchildren, and even their great-grandchildren and beyond would learn about *Money for Life*. During Bill's and Sally's lifetimes they could access the funds in the trust if they needed to, and when they die the trust documents, which they devise, will determine how the money is to be used.

Once the trust was established, Bill's and Sally's children recognized its value and began funding additional "banks" within the trust and building their own "banks" outside the trust. If the families continue to follow the practices of *Money for Life*, Bill's and Sally's grandchildren may never have to borrow from a commercial bank as long as they live.[72]

There are, of course, as many sets of circumstances as there are individuals and families. If you recall, John and Mary had a great plan to allow their money to care for them and their families while they were alive. They also established a dynasty trust that allowed them to pay forward to their children and grandchildren enough money to support a "banking" system for future generations.

---

71   A dynasty trust is one that continues in perpetuity, i.e., it never expires. This type of trust can create a "family bank" that is shared by multiple families derived from a single root over many generations. As you might expect, the longer the trust is in place the more money accrues in it and the more wealth passes from one generation to the next.

72   Dynasty trusts are complicated legal entities. I am not offering legal or tax advice. Consult an attorney or accountant before entering into any legal or tax related agreement.

Chapter 8 – "Show Me the Money"[73]

> "The truth is, there is money buried everywhere, and you have only to go to work to find it." ~ Henry David Thoreau

Three Secrets

There are three secrets to *Money for Life*.

- ☞ Finding the money... Is your money making you wealthy, or is it making the Behemoths rich and turning the Bureaucracies into fat cats? Look carefully at the paradigm that you have created to control your money. Examine the results that you get from that paradigm. Decide how you can restructure your personal economy.

- ☞ Knowing what to do with the money when you find it... recognizing that it is essential that *YouBeTheBank*. Until you are the "bank" you have, as Ben Franklin and Alexander Hamilton admonish, given up your liberty and made yourself a servant.

---

73 The famous line from the movie Jerry McGuire that professional football player Rod Tidwell (Cuba Gooding Jr.) shouted repeatedly in a phone exchange between him and his agent...Jerry Maguire (Tom Cruise).

> ☞ Knowing how to do what needs to be done...professionals in all occupations—from athletes to musicians and actors to politicians, business people, trades—people, and teachers—rely on the knowledge and insight of their coaches and guides to lead them to higher levels of doing what they do. It is no different with money.

Knowing the "secrets" is not, however, enough. You must also keep the benefits you derive from practicing *Money for Life* in the front of your mind...

> ☞ Freedom from debt-to-others
> ☞ Money when you need it because life has delivered the un-wanted or unexpected
> ☞ Income you don't have to work for but you won't outlive
> ☞ A legacy that you can pay forward to those you care about

Now, let's look at each of the three secrets separately and see how you can practice them in your own life starting today.

Finding the money

Finding the money is one of the most challenging processes of The *Money for Life* practices. Most Americans are so waterlogged with conventional wisdom that they never seriously consider their money management alternatives.

Many believe that they can solve money problems with a budget. Bud-geting is not the answer. Budgeting is a piece of the puzzle, but only a minor one; it looks at what is and projects today into the future. If what you are doing now isn't working, can you expect it to work better just because you project it into the future?

What The *Money for Life* Model teaches is a process of deconstructing and then reconstructing your personal economy so it works better today and lasts into the future — in good times and bad — as our examples in prior chapters demonstrated.

The best way to illustrate the first secret is by example. Here are the stories of a few people[74] who found the money to build their first "banks" by deconstructing their Debt Paradigm spending practices and reconstructing them using The *Money for Life* Model.

The Morning Latté

Joe and Joann are a couple in their early thirties with individual careers. They work in different parts of town, and both travel for work occasionally and participate in a wide range of after-hours professional and networking activities. This keeps their schedules in constant conflict. The one time that they had set aside exclusively for each other was their morning stop at a local coffee house for a latté and some pastries.

They typically spent fifteen or twenty dollars when they stopped, and felt that it was money well spent because it allowed them a relaxed chance to share the stories of their work and discuss personal and family issues that exhaustion from the daily grind kept them from doing in the evenings.

When Joe and Joann learned *Money for Life* however, they started looking at the mornings differently. As they deconstructed their money usage, they began to see the money they were spending at the coffee house as a $4,000.00 per year trap that they had set for themselves.

---

74 As is the case throughout this book, these people are fictional composites but represent real people who have used the strategies described in one form or another.

They recognized that they could have their coffee at home and use that money to start a "bank."

Since Joe and Joann began practicing *Money for Life,* they have paid off all of their debt and increased contributions to their "banks" to over $14,000.00 per year, without significantly changing their lifestyle.

Dinner Out

Jim and Jamie are an older, childless couple that met almost every evening after work at one of several favorite restaurants for cocktails and dinner. *Money for Life* taught them quickly that the $15,000.00 they were spending every year eating out was keeping several restaurateurs in pocket money but doing little for them. They loved fine dining, however, so they compromised.

Jim and Jamie attended cooking classes and found that their own creations were more than satisfactory. They also found that the joy of cooking together made their evenings even more enjoyable and that they could afford better wines for dinner at home than they could at the restaurant. Jim and Jamie still met once a week for dinner out. The net result was that they were able to start their first "banks" with about $12,000.00 a year.

The Family Vacation

Sam has two sons. When the boys were three and five, Sam had just begun practicing *Money for Life* and was planning the first family vacation. Sam had an idea; why not use the "banks" to fund some truly memorable vacations. Instead of package deals to amusement parks or resorts, why not take some inexpensive mini-vacations to state and national parks and put the money that they would have spent on more pricey trips into the "banks?"

The plan worked out quite well. The family put over $5,000.00 each year into a special "bank" to pay for a super vacation. In 5 years when the boys were 8 and 10, they all three went to Australia and New Zealand for almost a month. Over the next five years, they repaid the money they had borrowed for the Australian adventure and continued funding the "bank"; it grew to over $50,000.00. The boys were now 13 and 15 and the three of them traveled around the world with stops in Hawaii, Japan, Hong Kong, Seoul, Beijing and Moscow. Five years later — the boys were 18 and 20 — they visited South Africa, Israel, Turkey, Greece and Bermuda on the way home.

Finally, when both boys had graduated college, Sam gave them each a 90-day trip to Europe, which included a Euro Pass for rail travel, and enough money to stay in nice hotels and see whatever sights they wanted.

Today, the travel "bank" has over $150,000.00 in it and Sam and his new wife Samantha plan to use the money to visit South and Central America, take an African Safari, and follow their travel dreams as they grow old together.

The Private School

Susan, a very successful single mom, has three children who attended the first, second and fourth grades of a prestigious private school. Tuition was over $20,000.00 a year for the three of them, and parents typically made additional contributions of about $5,000.00 each year to the school. The tuition would increase annually based on the grade and general inflation.

When Susan began the practice of *Money for Life*, she decided to rethink the value of the education plan she was following. She found a highly regarded local public school system and moved into that district. The $25,000.00 that they saved by no longer paying tuition went into three "banks" — one for each child. Phyllis hired top students from the local high school (and later from the local college) to tutor her children as the need arose. When the children graduated from high school, each received academic scholarships to their colleges of choice and the "banks" paid for any shortfalls.

The story doesn't end there. When the children graduated from college and before they decided about graduate school, Susan sat down with each child and explained their "bank" in detail. She helped the children schedule a repayment plan for the education loans to make sure that their "bank" would survive, and taught them how to build bigger and better banks to serve them as they navigated life.

Each of Susan's children "got it." They took over their "banks" — each holding over $100,000.00 — and the now adult children practice *Money for Life* on their own. They will never have to borrow money from any commercial bank for items like cars, appliances, furniture and maybe even their homes.

The Dynasty Trust

Edward and Ellen are retired and have a comfortable but limited income. They wanted to create some sort of legacy for their grandchildren, but didn't know how to do that while maintaining their life style. Their *Money for Life* advisor helped them set up a dynasty trust as a "bank" to serve their grandchildren and future generations.

Edward and Ellen started a "bank" for each of their six grandchildren. They also set up a dynasty trust[75] to own and manage those "banks" in perpetuity after their deaths. The primary goal of the trust is to fund the "banks" of future generations and to manage the trust in accordance with the wishes that Edward and Ellen memorialized when they set up the trust.

Thanksgiving

George and Georgia have five children and eleven grandchildren. They are just a few years from transitioning from full time work to a more leisurely lifestyle. The five children and their families are scattered around the country but they all manage to come together at the family's mountain retreat for Thanksgiving week each year. Since the families of the children are still growing, however, it is becoming more challenging for them to afford the annual trip.

George and Georgia have the task of maintaining the facilities the families use each year when they come together and, as they looked forward to the limitations their own aging may impose, they decided to start a "bank" to support and maintain the family's tradition.

George and Georgia bought large whole life insurance policies that developed early cash values and each year would borrow (and repay during the ensuing 12 months) enough money to care for the property, and to assist their children with travel expenses. When George and Georgia

---

75 Search the internet for details about dynasty trusts and you will find links to many law firms and some articles. The author has researched the topic extensively and many of the law firm sites provide good information about dynasty trusts. Most, however, couch their discussions in terms of planning for the very wealthy. The cost of those kinds of trusts can be prohibitive. The author is currently working with a trust company to develop a simple dynasty trust that those who want to follow this strategy can easily access and use to set up a "bank" for their heirs.

die, the death benefit proceeds will be held in a trust devised specifically to take care of the property and to subsidize the travel of the children and their families and insure that the tradition continues.

Knowing what to do with the money when you find it

This book has pointed out the fallacies implicit in the current paradigm and in conventional wisdom. It has described the process and the practices of *Money for Life* in detail. It has also shown you ways to start a "bank" using a variety of financial products.

You might be surprised to learn that every suggestion made by the Behemoths in the financial industry — a group I have discounted to some extent throughout this book — is valid. What the Behemoths that sell investments do not make clear is that many — if not most — of those recommendations are valid only after you have a "bank" that fully supports your four pillars...

- ☞ Freedom from debt-to-others
- ☞ Money when you need it because life has delivered the unwanted or unexpected
- ☞ Income you don't have to work for but you won't outlive
- ☞ A legacy that you can pay forward to those you care about

You might also recall that just a few chapters ago you realized that no one has — until now — taught you about the practices that let YouBeTheBank or about the products that you can use to create your "bank" and bring all this power to your personal economy. With this in mind, reconsider the following:

- ☞ Would you agree: You have two roles to play when it comes to your money? One is the role of income producer in the vocation, career or business you have chosen. The other is to master *Money for Life* and become your own banker.

☞ Would you agree: It is just as important that you learn to be your own banker and master *Money for Life* as it is to learn what you need to do to succeed as an income producer?

☞ Would you agree: if you fail as your own banker, it could lead to failure as an income producer, failure as a provider, failure as a parent, failure as a spouse...that it is essential that you learn *Money for Life*?

Remember, when you answer "yes" to these questions

☞ you are rejecting the Debt Paradigm, which deceives you by promising that you can have everything you need and anything you want as long as you have enough "credit" (read as "debt" to you),

☞ you are accepting the principles of The *Money for Life* Model which says that you do not need debt-to-others. You can have everything you need and anything you want when you master *Money for Life* and become your own banker.

"Neither a borrower nor a lender be,
For loan oft loses both itself and friend,
And borrowing dulls the edge of husbandry.
This above all: to thine own self be true..." ~ William Shakespeare

Knowing how to do what needs to be done

During the past 30 years we have lost a lot of know-how that supported the common sense money practice of previous generations. The loss of the creativity that allowed our parents and grandparents to solve money problems and maintain peace of mind is, perhaps, the greatest of those losses. Add to that the innovation stifling regulation and compliance environment that plagues the entire financial services industry and the recipe produces a sterile and ineffective approach to solving your money problems.

The resulting conventional wisdom often manifests itself in software that produces packaged solutions in the guise of planning or advisory services. If you've ever gone through this process, you most likely received a professional looking binder — perhaps even a bound book — populated with charts, spreadsheets, illustrations, hypothetical performance projections, and graphs.

Somewhere in those pages you would have been pointed in the direction of the investment and insurance products and services of the company that developed your "plan." A series of disclaimers, which relieved the person who presented the proposal, and his Behemoth. from liability in all except the most egregious cases of misrepresentation or fraud, would have accompanied these recommendations.

As a case in point, you can refer to a previously referenced book: *Wall Street Versus America: The Rampant Greed and Dishonesty That Imperil Your Investments*.[76] The author, Mr. Gary Weiss, is a former reporter for Business Week and the author of *Born to Steal*, a book about Wall Street and the mob.

---

76 Wall Street Versus America: The Rampant Greed and Dishonesty That Imperil Your Investments by Gary Weiss, 290 pages, Portfolio.

This book's premise is that Wall Street's rules have been made to protect Wall Street from you, not the other way around. That those who preside over institutions like the New York Stock Exchange and the Securities and Exchange Commission and FINRA [formerly the NASD (National Association of Securities Dealers)] have perfected the art of sounding indignant but doing nothing.

His book opens in 2004 with a Kafkaesque dispute between Merrill Lynch, Pierce, Fenner & Smith Inc., and a man named Rand Groves who went from "paper millionaire" to "thousandaire" to "hundredaire" to "nothingaire" with the help of his Merrill Lynch adviser.

The case came complete with persuasive evidence that the adviser had written a postdated note to cover his tracks. But the case also went through a slanted (according to Mr. Weiss) Wall Street arbitration process in which the plaintiff didn't have a chance. As Mr. Groves was later told by a securities lawyer: "Is it raining outside? You have a better chance of being struck by lightning than winning this case."

This story is not meant to indict individual advisors. It reflects on the process, however, that forces advisors to limit their suggestions to those approved by the FINRA through their companies, and which focus more on preventing lawsuits than solving your money problems.

There is hope, however. Many Certified Financial Planning Practitioners® meticulously follow the rules set by the regulators, but don't limit their recommendations to those regurgitated by a piece of software designed primarily to prevent some financial Behemoth from being sued. In addition, many insurance professionals eschew securities licenses altogether. These advisors offer solutions that do not rely exclusively on risk-based products, and refer the clients who have investment needs to a qualified independent investment advisor.

It is well beyond the scope of this first book to address each situation in which being your own "bank" can serve you better than relying on the alternatives conventional wisdom puts forth. You need a professional advisor who is skilled in and knowledgeable about *Money for Life* practices to help you make informed decisions that are in your best interest.

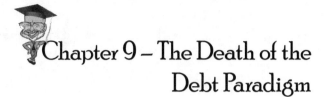

Chapter 9 – The Death of the Debt Paradigm

In the Preface and Introduction to this book we observed that America is in the throes of a financial breakdown. The severe credit problems of both individuals — especially the oldest of our citizens — and institutions are evidence of this.

America is roiling in credit card and other consumer debt. The subprime mortgage market is in its death throes. The credit markets around the world are collapsing in on themselves, making even reasonably qualified credit applications for legitimate borrowers hard to come by.

A bit later we discussed a financial behavior model I call the Debt Paradigm that is the underpinning of current American thinking about money. It aims to convince you that you can have everything you need and anything you want as long as you have enough credit.

The Debt Paradigm tells you this about money: earn, borrow, spend, repay, repeat that cycle endlessly, and, as an afterthought, bank some so you can spend it later.

Next you learned about The *Money for Life* Model, which makes a subtle and essential change to the failed Debt Paradigm, when it introduces the *Money for Life* ideas that let YouBeTheBank.

You can operate your personal economy using the same practices that banks and many silently wealthy individuals use, and create the same results they do; practices that are the foundation of every fortune — no matter how small or large:

☞ Get money — earn it, inherit it, win the lottery, sell "stuff," invent (just don't rob the bank)

☞ Bank it – put it someplace that will allow you to act as your own "bank"

☞ Borrow from your "bank"

☞ Spend what you borrow to buy the things you need and want

☞ Repay your "bank" both the principal you borrowed and the interest on the money you borrowed

While the Debt Paradigm teaches you to Earn, Borrow from others, Spend, Repay others and maybe save a little for the future. The *Money for Life* Model trains you to: *Earn, Bank, Borrow* from your "bank," *Spend, Repay Yourself and Recapture* all of the money that flows through your life in your own "banks."

The first step is to look carefully at the preconceptions — called shibboleths — that you carry around in your mind and that pop up like unwanted ads on your computer every time you are about to make a money decision.

Money for Life is an old paradigm made new by innovative 21st century thinking and the failure of the current paradigm to help individuals and families. *Money for Life* demonstrates that you need the foundation and the Four Pillars that are the bulwark of wealth, regardless of the size of your estate or your starting point:

☞ live free from debt-to-others.

☞ create income you don't have to work for and you can't out-live.

☞ make sure you have money when you need it when a life event causes a loss of income or unexpected expenses arise for things like health care or long-term care.

☞ assure that you can pay forward your wealth and wisdom to your children, grandchildren, and every generation that follows you, as long as America stands as the beacon of freedom and free enterprise that the world has looked to for leadership for the past two centuries.

Using real situations where folks were successful applying the *Money for Life* concepts and practices described in this book, you learned that every person or couple can succeed if they employ these practices in the management of their money.

We discussed in some detail the various places you could put your "banking" money:

☞ savings accounts or certificates of deposit at someone else's bank

☞ investments like mutual funds

☞ your 401(k)

☞ dividend paying whole life insurance from a mutual company

☞ other forms of life insurance

and why using mutual whole life insurance works best in this paradigm.

What now?

I would love to be able to deliver "the answer" to individual questions in this book. That simply isn't possible. Every person and family has unique questions and unique answers.

If you are like most who have encountered the *Money for Life* concept and who decide to build an enduring financial structure and your own "bank," you will need a practitioner:

- ☞ who understands the *Money for Life* system
- ☞ has the experience needed to advise you as you deconstruct your current money structure, replace the failed Debt Paradigm and reconstruct a unique money and wealth paradigm
- ☞ can assist you in choosing and applying for the insurance products needed to implement your program
- ☞ commits to guide you as the years pass and your situation changes.

If you wish to learn more about the process and products that you can use to make this powerful set of practices a part of your life, you can visit www.YouBeTheBank.com where you will find lots of information, and an information request form you can use if you don't see the information you need. The staff at the web site will do its best to answer your questions, introduce you to an advisor in your area, if that's what's needed, and link you to other resources that might be helpful to you in your quest for a Personal Economy that lasts...in good times and bad.

Read on...and best wishes for success in building a *Money for Life* "bank" for YOUR MONEY!

Appendix – A

The Dazzling Dozen

Twelve Reasons why you [and other money smart people] should choose to build a personal economy that lets YouBeTheBank and that lasts in good times and bad:

1. You can get to the money in your "bank" whenever you want it or need it…no penalties, no waiting, no taxes.

2. The government, your employer, or any other outsiders have nothing to say about how you operate your "bank."

3. Your "bank" is protected from creditors and lawsuits. [77]

4. You can borrow against your "bank" for any reason and you don't have to qualify in any way.

5. When you do borrow from your "bank," the money in your "bank" keeps growing as if you hadn't borrowed a cent… your money does double duty.

6. Your "bank" allows you to recover the money you pay to purchase cars, household furnishings, vacations and other big ticket items or to fund education, business start-ups or any other costly expense, and deposit both principal and interest you recover right back into your "bank."

---

77 This document does not provide legal advice. Protections are not the same in every state and may not be available in some states. Consult an attorney about the laws in your state.

7. Your "bank" allows you to put all of the interest you would normally pay to credit card companies, banks and other credit grantors into your "bank" where it compounds for your benefit.

8. Your "bank" allows you to pre-pay the cost of future health and long-term care so the money you need as you age is in your "bank" when you need it most.

9. Your "bank" funds an inflation-protected income that you do not have to work for and you can't outlive.

10. You can use the money in your "bank" when an unforeseen life event throws you off track. (and that happens to everyone at some time or another.)

11. Your "bank" lets you grow your wealth tax free every year... no sliding backward...no worries about stock market crashes or real estate market bubbles...just peace of mind about your money.

12. Your "bank" serves you without compromise while you are alive and allows you to pay forward — tax free and to anyone you choose — your legacy of wealth and wisdom.

Appendix – B Why Budgets Don't Work

> "The trouble with a budget is that it's hard to fill up one hole without digging another." ~ Dan Bennett

A traditional budget claims to both predict and control your money usage. It does not, however, serve well as a primary money management tool. It can be helpful as a tracking device, but instead of liberating you from conventional wisdom it tends to…

- ☞ enslave you — so you want to escape
- ☞ crystallize your thinking — so you stop thinking altogether
- ☞ and solidify your money usage patterns — so you can't see your alternatives.

The Four Pillars

Money for Life employs a more holistic approach to capturing and evaluating information about your personal money usage patterns. The practice called *Take the Mystery Out of Money* allows you to measure your progress against the Four Pillars of financial security:

- ☞ The first pillar — freedom from debt-to-others
- ☞ The second pillar — money when you need it to replace lost income or because expected and unexpected life events such as job loss, medical expense, home care or nursing home costs put you in a financial bind
- ☞ The third pillar — an income you don't have to work for and you won't outlive
- ☞ The fourth pillar — a legacy of wealth and wisdom for those you care about

Take the Mystery Out of Money

Take the Mystery Out of Money guides you as you answer two sets of questions that are critical to achieve success as the master of your money:

13. What is My True Net Worth?
    - What do I own?
    - What do I owe?

14. What's Left for Me?
    - What do I earn?
    - Where does it go?

To answer these questions is not all that easy. I do not recommend that you approach this exercise alone. You'll better serve your own best interest if you engage an experienced guide to help you navigate this process.

Initially your guide will walk you through this process. You'll also want to go through this exercise with your guide whenever you are about to make a significant money decision and on a scheduled monthly or quarterly basis. When you are entirely comfortable with this exercise and feel confident, you can do it on your own.

Each exercise uses a spreadsheet. You can find an example of each at the end of this discussion. In the next few pages you will learn more about how to use these forms both by explanation and by example.

What is My True Net worth?
—What do I own?

Material items

When a commercial bank asks you for financial information it wants to know every detail — furniture, jewelry, appliances, electronics, etc. — and it wants to know the price or value of these material items. The banker will also ask about your debt-to-others and your other assets. The banker will subtract what you owe from the guesstimated value of what you own and interpret this as your net worth. This is not your True Net Worth.

Take the Mystery Out of Money looks at material items that you use on a regular basis as valueless — furniture, clothing, computer equipment, garden tools…you get the picture. If you would have to replace an item because it was damaged or just wore out, that item is ignored. Items that would bring only pennies on the dollar if you sold them are also ignored. Don't include these items on the list of what you own.

The exceptions to this rule are items, such as automobiles and real property that may have a net value but are tied directly to a loan. You should also include items with real value — perhaps rare coins or a collection of Civil War memorabilia — that you would not intend to replace if you sold them and that have real and significant value in the market.

Therefore, when you respond to the question "What do I own?" only include the material items that you could or would sell, and that would fetch enough money to eliminate debt-to-others and make a positive difference in your life and lifestyle if you sold them.

Financial products

In addition to material items, you may also own some financial products such as cash value life insurance, annuities, savings accounts, certificates of deposit, IRA's, 401(k)'s, stocks, bonds, mutual funds, and so on. You may also have an interest in a small business. All of these belong on the list of what you own.

Valuing what you own

Much of the challenge of this part of the exercise lies in placing values on the material and some of the financial products. The savings type of financial product is easy to evaluate since it has a guaranteed value. The $10,000.00 CD at your credit union is worth $10,000.00.

A natural tendency might be, however, to over-value material items; your house, car, time share interest, and so on. You might also trick yourself into crystallizing the value of your investments such as IRA's, mutual funds and the like, which are, by their very nature, at risk of losing value. You'll want to avoid these two very serious errors. Your guide is your most valuable resource during this part of the process.

What is my True Net Worth?
— What do I owe?

Art and science

The second key element in calculating your True Net Worth is your debt-to-others — what you owe. Advanced *Take the Mystery Out of Money* practices incorporate an algorithm that adds a portion of the projected known cost of debt-to-others into what you owe. For this exercise at this level, however, you'll want simply to list your debts.

Debts

If a debt-to-others is directly tied to an item you listed as one that you own — your car, house, a 401(k) loan, etc. — then you'll list the amount you owe next to the amount you put in the "What I own" column and record the difference in the "Net Value to Me" column. Record the difference as a positive number if the value is greater than the debt-to-others or a negative number if the opposite is true.

Entries in the debt-to-others column that do not relate directly to items you own, e.g., credit card debt, are recorded as negative numbers in the "Net Value to Me" column.

Assets

Transfer entries in the "What I Own" column that have no corresponding entries in the "Debt-to-others" column, e.g., a savings account, into "Net Value to Me" column as positive numbers.

Once you have honestly recorded all of these numbers your True Net Worth will be the total of the "Net Value to Me" column.

There is one more column on this from — "Future Cost of Debt-to-Others." If you'd like to feel what your future holds under the Debt Paradigm, you can calculate the interest that lies in your future and enter it in this column. If you continue managing your money according to the dictates of conventional wisdom this may represent your future True Net Worth.

True Net Worth				
Description	What Do I Own	What Do I Owe	Net Value to Me	Future Cost of Debt-to-Others

What's Left for Me?
— What do I earn?

Watch out for this

If you thought you could easily fool yourself — and perhaps a banker or two — while determining your True Net Worth, then you will be amazed at how easy it is to trick yourself when you look at your earnings and expenses. True Net Worth is a snap shot of a slow moving train. "What's Left for Me," the bottom line of this exercise, is a snippet from the video of a jet flying at Mach II.

The ghost

> "The average family exists only on paper and its average budget is a fiction, invented by statisticians for the convenience of statisticians." ~ Sylvia Porter

Earnings are a phantom. Every penny that enters into and passes through your life is included in our discussion of "earnings," but you never see a great portion of that money. Rather than using abstract explanations for this part of the process — because it is so unique to each person and family — let's take a look at a typical American's paycheck.

Who was that masked man

> "What is the difference between a taxidermist and a tax collector? The taxidermist takes only your skin." ~ Mark Twain

Let's say you earn $5,000.00 per month. The first thing that happens to your money is that the Federal Government takes its share — 15%

to 25% or $750.00 to $1,250.00. Then the same federal government takes 7.65% for Social Security and Medicare. That's another $382.50. That leaves you with $3,867.50 to $3367.50.

Perhaps that's a partially untrue statement, however, since the state, county and city may take their piece of your pie before you get a chance to cash your check. In some few states that's nothing or a pittance; for most it's another 5% — $250.00 or more.

The incredible shrinking paycheck

> "The Eiffel Tower is the Empire State Building after taxes." ~ Dr Agon Fly

Now your paycheck has shrunk to between $3,617.50 and $3117.50. And, you have not yet paid any of your bills, saved any money for the expected ups and downs of life — much less the unexpected — or put any money aside for the education of your children or for your own retirement. Even the self employed who write their own paychecks face these same challenges.

In addition to wages that are taxed, many — if not most — Americans receive other income from savings and investments. These amounts are not usually taxed directly but must be added in at tax time each year.

Where does it go?

For simplicity sake we'll assume no additional income and use $3,400.00, which is about halfway between the two after tax amounts, as the basis for the next part of our discussion.

Another masked man – so soon

The first thing that happens to the net pay of most Americans is that it's further diminished by a series of payroll deductions for "benefits," with health insurance at about $250.00[78] and 401(k) contributions at about $300.00[79] leading the list. Again, for simplicity sake, we'll refer collectively to these as "benefits" in our example and use $400.00 as the combined amount that covers both. That leaves you with $3,000.00 — about 60% of your gross pay before you get out the door of your workplace.

Home at last

When you leave work and go home, the first thing you have to take care of is home itself. The 30 year $165,000.00 fixed mortgage on your single family home at 7% will run you about $1,100.00, leaving you with $1,900.00. Subtract from that amount the taxes ($100.00), insurance ($50.00), phone ($60.00), utilities ($130.00), cable or dish ($75.00), and maintenance ($110.00) that are part and parcel of the typical home, and you are left with $1,375.00.

Zoom, zoom, zoom

Your car costs money too. Conservatively you'll send about $250.00 to some lender for a payment monthly (guess who's getting richer) and another $125.00 to your insurance company. An oil company will sell

---

78   2005 results reported by the National Coalition on Health Care, 1200 G Street, NW, Suite 750, Washington, DC.

79   Employee Benefits Research Institute, 2121 K Street, NW, Suite 600, Washington, DC.

you gasoline and oil changes and you'll go through a car wash once or twice — that's $150.00 more. That leaves you with $850.00.

Let's eat

Now, let's go shopping. Groceries will cost you about $450.00 each month; lunches at work another $240.00; date night once each week (Dutch treat) $120.00 per month (cheap date); limited wardrobe enhancements at $40.00 (cheap wardrobe, too) — and you're out of money! You have not even begun to consider the occasional latte`, a vacation, the emergency room visit, poker night with friends, tickets to your favorite sporting event, the loan your brother, sister or cousin needs, and on, and on, and on...

Description	(+) What Do I Earn?	(-) Taxes Withheld	(-)Benefits Withheld	(-) Take Home Pay	(-) Expenses	(=) What's Left
	$5000	1600	400	3000	—	3000
Mortgage					1100	1900
Property Taxes					100	1800
H.O. Ins.					50	1750
Phone					60	1690
Utilities					130	1560
Cable					75	1485
Maint.					110	1375
Car Loan					250	1125
Car Ins.					125	1000
Gas & Oil					150	850
Groceries					450	400
Eating Out					240	160
Date Night					120	40
Wardrobe					40	0

What's Left For Me? (Example)

No money left for the latté, a vacation, the emergency room visit, poker night with friends, tickets to sporting events, the loan a relative needs and on and on and on.

"I'm living so far beyond my income that we may almost be said to be living apart." ~ William Cowper

The three stooges

So what happens next? One of three common scenarios emerges when folks discover that their incomes are not big enough (or their expenses are too big). The first is to eliminate items that are considered non-essential. For many, that means they drop their health and life insurance and/or their 401(k)/IRA contributions and items like home maintenance so they can enhance their lifestyle.

When this approach falls short — and it usually does — the second, and equally as common "solution" to the dilemma of not-enough-income is more debt-to-others; credit cards first, followed by second mortgages or equity lines of credit, refinancing the house…you get the picture.

The third common option is adopting an austerity program: rice and beans at every meal, carry your lunch, take the bus to work, cut out the TV subscription service, only shop at discount stores and thrift shops, and so on. This approach actually works better than the others. Its biggest drawback is that it is not sustainable over the long run. As soon as the financial pressure is off there is a tendency to "reward" oneself for having succeeded and to slip right back into the commonly accepted practices of the Debt Paradigm.

The bottom line

Take the Mystery Out of Money does not, of course, recommend the approaches that conventional wisdom suggests. The aim of *Take the Mystery Out of Money* is to deconstruct your money usage patterns and reconstruct them so they better serve you and your goals.

Once you have honestly filled in the *Take the Mystery Out of Money* spreadsheets with all of your income and expenses — whether you have a surplus or not — your guide will help you discover omissions (unrecognized income from savings or retirement plans for example) and recognize distortions (overvalued assets or unrecognized expense such as participation fees for the kids sports programs) so you can complete the deconstruct/reconstruct process, begin to build your "bank" and escape the dungeon of the Debt Paradigm.

The final curtain

> "Rather go to bed supperless than rise in debt." ~ Benjamin Franklin

This phase of *Take the Mystery Out of Money* is where you have to decide: are you committed to controlling the money that flows through your life and becoming the master of your money or are you willing to continue to allow government and the sellers of products — financial as well as consumer goods — to control your money and your future? It's a long question in words but your answer is short — door number 1 or door number 2?

My guess is that having read this book you will choose to build a personal economy that lasts...in good times and bad by following the *Money for Life* model.

Choosing a guide

If you do not currently have a guide that you rely on, please visit www.YouBeTheBank.com and request an introduction to a recognized *Money for Life* advisor.

Best wishes

Good luck with your adventure. If you honestly follow this exciting path you will have a new and improved way to control the money that flows through your life and a powerful new ally in your quest for the peace of mind that comes with true wealth.

Appendix – C

The following article is instructive because it describes the similarities between insurance and banking and gives insight into why the insurance industry has been able to consistently deliver services to its customers — even during the Great Depression — by taking the difficult long-term view needed to protect those customers and deliver on the promise of cash value insurance.

This scholarly and detailed report is particularly instructive today as the banking community is once again shaken by its willingness to take risks — this time on sub-prime mortgages — that the insurance industry has avoided.

The Banking and Insurance Holidays of 1933
Thomas F. Huertas and Joan L. Silverman.[80]

During 1933 there were two financial holidays, one in banking and one in life insurance. The first is well known. The Banking Holiday shut down every bank in the United States for ten days and ushered in sweeping changes in banking regulation.

The second holiday is practically unknown, even to historians of insurance, who either ignore it or gloss over it. The "insurance holiday" suspended the payment of cash surrender values and the granting of

---

80   The bulk this article has been omitted for brevity sake. The entire article and notes can be found at http://www.thebhc.org/publications/BEHprint/v013/p0105-p0115. pdf.

policy loans for a period of nearly six months. However, this holiday had no regulatory repercussions, although it affected millions of Americans, and it stemmed from the same cause as the banking holiday — the Depression.

This paper contrasts the two holidays. It starts with a discussion of the similarities between banking and insurance. The paper then describes the cause and consequences of the two holidays. A concluding section draws some inferences about the regulatory process.

The Similarity Between Banking and Insurance

Banks and insurance companies perform very similar economic functions. Both are financial intermediaries. Each receives money —deposits or premiums — from people or businesses who wish to save and lends it to people and businesses that wish to borrow. This is risk management pure and simple.

The difference between banking and insurance lies solely in the customer's claim on the institution. The depositor has an unconditional right to withdraw his funds at maturity. In the ease of a checking account he can do so on demand. In contrast, the insurance policyholder has no such right. His claim is conditional. He has no claim unless and until the event insured against actually occurs -- a fire, an accident, or death.

In the case of life insurance, the similarities with banking are closer. Except for term insurance, life insurance products contain savings and credit features. For example, a whole-life policy includes not only insurance, but also provides a tax-deferred savings account and allows the policyholder to borrow against the cash value of the policy. Thus, "a life insurance company performs some of the functions of a savings bank and, to a smaller degree, of a commercial bank."

Bibliography

Alumpur, Gopala. *Die Broke & Wealthy, The Insurance Bonanza that Beats the Taxman While You're Still Alive.* Toronto: Chestnut Publishing Group, 2003.

Augar, Phillip. *The Greed Merchants: How Investment Banks Played the Free Market Game.* New York: Penquin Group, 2005.

Bach, David. *The Automatic Millionaire.* New York: Broadway Books/Random House, 2004.

Baldwin, Ben G. *The New Life Insurance Investment Advisor.* New York: McGraw-Hill, 2002.

Biggs, Barton. *Hedge Hogging.* Hoboken, NJ: John Wiley & Sons, Inc., 2006.

Black, Kenneth and Harold D. Skipper, Jr. *Life & Health Insurance.* New Jersey: Prentice Hall, 2000.

Black, William K. *The Best Way to Rob a Bank Is to Own One.* Austin: University of Texas Press, 2005.

Bogle, John C. *"The Amazing Disappearance of The Individual Stockholder."* Wall Street Journal, October 3, 2005.
  —, *The Battle for the Soul of Capitalism.* New Haven: Yale University Press, 2005.

—, "The Emperor's New Mutual Funds." *Wall Street Journal*, July 8, 2003.

—, "Fair Shake or Shakedown." *Wall Street Journal*, July 8, 2004.

—, " How Mutual Funds Lost Their Way." *Wall Street Journal*, June 20, 2000.

—, "Specialist Man." *Wall Street Journal*, September 19, 2003.

Bonner, William, *Financial Reckoning Day*. Hoboken, NJ: John Wiley & Sons, 2003.

Bonner, William and Wiggin, Addison, *Empire of Debt: The Rise of an Epic Financial Crisis*. Hoboken, NJ: John Wiley & Sons, 2006.

Callahan, Gene, *Economics for Real People*. Auburn, AL: Ludwig von Mises Institute, 2004.

Chancellor, Edward. *Devil Take The Hindmost: A History of Financial Speculation*. New York: The Penquin Group, 1999.

Chernow, Ron. *The House of Morgan, An American Banking Dynasty and the Rise of Modern Finance*. New York: Simon & Schuster, 1990.

Clason, George S., *The Richest Man in Babylon*. New York: Signet 1988.

Cole, Mark Benjamin. *The Pied Pipers of Wall Street: How Analysts Sell You Down the River*. Princeton, NJ: Bloomberg Press, 2001.

Dyke, Barry James, *The Pirates of Manhattan*. Portsmouth, NH: 555 Publishing, 2007.

Franklin, Benjamin – *The Way to Wealth with Comments by Dr Agon Fly*. Denver, CO: Poor Richard Publishing Company, 2008.

Griffin, G. Edward, *The Creature from Jekyll Island*. Westlake Village, CA: American Media, 2004.

Josephson, Matthew. *The Robber Barons*. New York: Harcourt Brace & Company, 1934, 1964.

Kelly, Tom. *The New Reverse Mortgage Formula, How to Convert Home Equity Into Tax-Free Income*. New York: John Wiley & Sons, 2005.

Kindleberger, Charles P. *Manias, Panics and Crashes*. New York: John Wiley & Sons, 2000.

Leimberg, Steve and Robert J. Doyle, Jr. "Tools and Techniques of Life Insurance Planning." *The National Underwriter*, 2004.

Linn, Kurt. *The Trouble with Mutual Funds*. Seattle: Elton-Wolff Publishing, 2002.

Lowenstein, Roger. *Origins of the Crash, the Great Bubble and Its Undoing*. New York: The Penquin Press, 2004.

Lubeck, Walter, *The Tao of Money*. Twin Lakes, WI: Lotus Press, 2000.

Mackay, Charles, *Extraordinary Popular Delusions & the Madness of Crowds*. New York: Three Rivers Press, 1980.

Malkiel, Burton G. *A Random Walk Down Wall Street*. New York: W.W. Norton & Company, 2007.

Mrkvicka, Edward Jr. *Your Bank Is Ripping You Off*. New York: St. Martin Press, 1999.

Nash, R. Nelson. *Becoming Your Own Banker – The Infinite Banking Concept*. Birmingham, AL: Infinite Banking Concepts, 2000.

Palast, Greg. *The Best Democracy Money Can Buy. An Investigative Reporter Exposes the Truth About Globalization, Corporate Cons and High Finance Fraudsters*. Sterling VA: Pluto Press, 2002.

Paulson, Paul, *Money and the Middle Man*. Parker, CO: Outskirts Press, 2005.

Reingold, Dan. *Confessions of a Wall Street Analyst*. New York: Harper Collins, 2006.

Rogers, George L., *Benjamin Franklin's The Art of Virtue – His Formula for Successful Living*. Midvale, Utah: George L. Rogers, 1996.

Slott, Ed. *The Retirement Savings Time Bomb...And How to Defuse It*. New York: Penguin Group, 2003.

Smith, Adam, *The Wealth of Nations*. New York: Bantam Classics

Swensen, David F. *Unconventional Success: A Fundamental Approach to Personal Investment*. New York: Simon & Schuster, 2005.

Weber, Richard M. *Revealing Life Insurance Secrets, How the Pros Pick, Design and Evaluate Their Own Policies*. Ellicott City, MD: Marketplace Books, 2005.

Weiss, Gary. *Wall Street Versus America, The Rampant Greed and Dishonesty That Imperils Your Investments*. New York: Penguin Group, 2006.

Winslow, Edward. *Blind Faith, Our Misplaced Trust in the Stock Market and Smarter, Safer Ways to Invest*. San Francisco: Berrett-Koehler, 2003.

Wright, Robert E. and Cohen, David J., *The Financial Founding Fathers*. Chicago: The University of Chicago Press, 2006.

Young, Thomas W. *Life Insurance: Will It Pay When I Die?* Beaver, PA: Personality Press, 2005.

Index

Notes

Notes

Notes

Notes

Notes

Notes

Notes

Notes

Notes

About Dr Agon Fly...

Dr Agon Fly speaks for the professionals who are *Money for Life* advocates. Dr Agon Fly is real...not as a flesh and blood person like you. However, Dr Agon Fly embodies the hundreds and thousands of women and men who have contributed to the development — over decades, centuries and millennia — of the humanizing ideas and values that you encounter when you explore *Money for Life...in good times and bad.*

When Dr Agon Fly speaks to you, it is with this myriad of voices...voices that have spoken in unison forever; voices that have survived every kind of challenge; voices that are now raised to help you challenge your Debt Paradigm...and overcome.

About Jeffrey Reeves BA, MA...

Jeffrey Reeves is a licensed life insurance agent and was formerly a registered securities rep. He has been guiding clients for over 30 years as they chart their paths to financial security. During this time clients, insurance professionals and financial advisors have all contributed ideas, strategies and tactics to the arsenal of tools that emerge throughout *Money for Life...in good times and bad.*

These contributions offer the reader an extraordinary wealth of insight, knowledge and just plain old common sense about money.

Although creativity allowed these ideas to come together as a coherent message, they remain the common property of dedicated advisors and guides. I encourage everyone who deals with their clients' money to pay heed. The authors wish you well in your quest.